Authenticity, Identity, and Being Yourself at Work

HBR Work Smart Series

*Rise faster with quick reads,
real stories, and expert advice.*

It's not easy to navigate the world of work when you're exploring who you are and what you want in life. How do you translate your interests, skills, and education into building a career you love?

The **HBR Work Smart Series** features the topics that matter to you most in your early career, including being yourself at work, collaborating with (sometimes difficult) colleagues and bosses, managing your mental health, and weighing major job decisions. Each title includes chapter recaps and links to video, audio, and more. The HBR Work Smart books are your practical guides to stepping into your professional life and moving forward with confidence.

Books in the series include:

Authenticity, Identity, and Being Yourself at Work

Bosses, Coworkers, and Building Great Work Relationships

Boundaries, Priorities, and Finding Work-Life Balance

Experience, Opportunity, and Developing Your Career

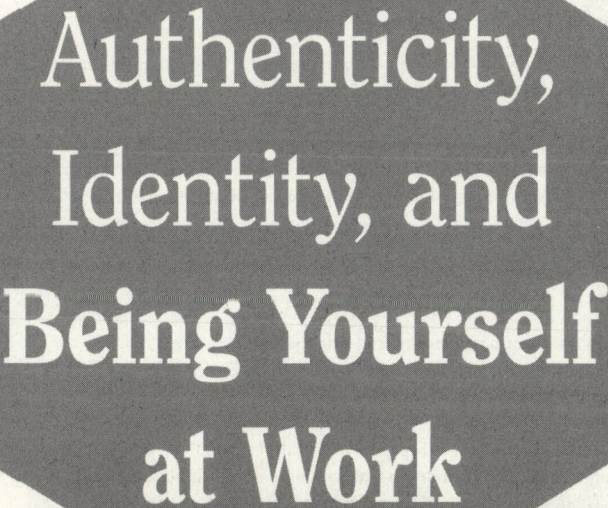

WORK SMART

Tips for Navigating Your Career

Authenticity, Identity, and Being Yourself at Work

HARVARD BUSINESS REVIEW PRESS

Boston, Massachusetts

Printed in India by Replika Press Pvt. Ltd.

10 9 8 7 6 5 4 3

The web addresses referenced in this book were live and correct at the time of the book's publication but may be subject to change.

Library of Congress Cataloging-in-Publication Data

Title: Authenticity, identity, and being yourself at work.
Description: Boston, Massachusetts : Harvard Business Review Press, [2024] | Series: HBR work smart series
Identifiers: LCCN 2023048549 (print) | LCCN 2023048550 (ebook) | ISBN 9781647827021 (paperback) | ISBN 9781647827038 (epub)
Subjects: LCSH: Honesty in the workplace. | Self-disclosure. | Authenticity (Philosophy) | Communication in organizations. | Corporate culture. | Work environment.
Classification: LCC HF5549.5.H66 A984 2024 (print) | LCC HF5549.5.H66 (ebook) | DDC 650.1—dc23/eng/20231228
LC record available at https://lccn.loc.gov/2023048549
LC ebook record available at https://lccn.loc.gov/2023048550

ISBN: 978-1-64782-702-1
eISBN: 978-1-64782-703-8

FSC

MIX
Paper | Supporting
responsible forestry
FSC™ C016779
www.fsc.org

CONTENTS

Introduction: Authenticity and the Power of You   xi
You are the sum of all your parts. Honor them.
by Madison Butler

SECTION 1

Understanding the Authentic You

1. Getting Comfortable Being Yourself at Work   3
   It's easier said than done.
   by Lan Nguyen Chaplin

2. How to Find, Define, and Use Your Values   15
   They should reflect the most important aspects
   of your life.
   by Irina Cozma

SECTION 2

Communicating Authentically, Without Oversharing

3. Using Authentic Conversation to Connect
   with Others   25
   Form relationships that feel productive,
   not draining.
   by Susan McPherson

4. **My Pronouns Are They/Them. What Are Yours?**   31
   Sharing how you identify, from introductions
   to correcting others.
   An interview with Lily Zheng by Paige Cohen

5. **Self-Disclosure at Work**   39
   How much should you reveal about your personal life?
   An interview with Katherine W. Phillips by Amanda Kersey

6. **Should You Disclose an Invisible Marginalized
   Identity at Work?**   47
   What to consider before making the call.
   by Dannie Lynn Fountain

7. **Coming Out as Trans at Work**   57
   A framework for before, during, and after.
   by Michael Cherny, Shalene Gupta, and Sandra J. Sucher

SECTION 3

Dealing with Real Emotions

8. **Managing the Hidden Stress of Emotional Labor**   75
   Concealing your true feelings is exhausting.
   by Susan David

9. **Do You Ever Second-Guess Yourself?**   81
   Five tips to help you combat imposter syndrome.
   by Tucci Ivowi

10. **Your Job and Your Identity Are
    Two Different Things**   89
    Don't conflate your role with self-worth.
    by Tim O'Brien

11. **So, You Cried at Work**   95
Bounce back with grace.
by Melody Wilding

SECTION 4

When Identity and Work Collide

12. **When You Don't Feel Comfortable
Being Yourself at Work**   105
There may be more leeway for self-expression
than you think.
by Dorie Clark

13. **Why the Model Minority Myth Is So Harmful**   111
You shouldn't have to perform for anyone.
by Janice Omadeke

14. **My Colleagues Can't Get My Name Right**   123
It's about them—not you.
by Talisa Lavarry

15. **How to Have Difficult Conversations
Without Burning Bridges**   133
Confronting others when they go against your values.
by Evelyn Nam

16. **Are You Living a Double Life on Social Media?**   143
Redefining what "professional" means on LinkedIn.
by Paige Cohen

Notes   151
Index   155
About the Contributors   161

Authenticity and the Power of You

by Madison Butler

It took me 25 years to know the meaning of my name and recognize the sound of my own voice. During the formative years of my life, I believed that the authentic version of myself was the weakest part of myself.

For so long my name sounded like something from an unspoken language when it left my mouth. I followed my name with question marks, unsure of who I was: Was I the parts I showed the world? Or the things that haunted me as I tried to sleep at night? Was I the best things I've ever done, or the accumulation of my worst mistakes?

All of the above.

I am a Black, queer, neurodivergent woman, and that combination is my superpower. But for a long time I viewed these things as weaknesses. I was told that I had to be anyone *but* myself in order to be seen as worthy. I tried at every turn to run from myself. I straightened my hair until it fell out, changed my voice, dressed the part, loved who I thought I was supposed to love—except myself.

In my early twenties, my fear of who I truly was led me to situations that put me in danger because I was unwilling to see the value in my own life, body, and identity. It took almost dying for me to see the heart of who I was, and to be open to meeting myself for the first time.

Meeting myself was like meeting the love I had always chased and finding the friendship I had always searched for.

What if I told you the parts of yourself that you feel shame about are the most powerful parts of you? Would you believe me, a complete stranger, in the lines of a book?

Who Am I?

This question lives in the back of many people's minds, slipping further from consciousness year to year as we learn to assimilate to the wants of the world around us. But knowing yourself is more than knowing your favorite foods or your favorite childhood memories. We are all made of complex identities, experiences, and lenses that impact how we navigate the spaces we inhabit.

From a young age so many of us—especially women, people of color, LGBTQ+ individuals, and any other identities that are not in the majority—are told that to be valuable, we must change. So we morph into what we think our parents want, our teachers want, our organizations want, our society wants—every day stepping further from our true selves. We rarely have time to ask, "Who am I really? Who do I want to be?"

Authenticity is who we are at our core—the things that make us whole, the things that make us scream into the void, the love that fills our bellies. We are not compartmentalized beings; we are the sum of all our parts. We are our identities, our values, our traumas, our happiest memories, and our worst moments. And we deserve to honor all of these parts, even the ones that have been living in the shadows.

Authenticity at Work

In recent years, companies have adopted the concept of authenticity as a culture-related buzzword. They have used the concept to hire new candidates or have put it into their "core values" without a full exploration of what it means. They try to allow employees to be comfortable . . . as long as people don't step too far outside the lines of "normal." But there is no normal. There are only parameters created by society.

We are told we have to have a work self, a family self, a friend self, a partner self, and so on. I'll let you in on a little secret, though: Those are all the same person. You cannot check your humanity at the door of your organization, and your company should not expect that of you. We do our best work when we are given the space and the safety to exist wholly in our identities, our quirks, and our experiences.

We must ask ourselves what makes us feel happy and safe, and then regularly edit our lives to reflect our needs, desires, and safety. When you aim to make everyone happy, not only will you end up exhausted, but you will remain in environments that no longer serve you. Too often we stay at jobs or in relationships with

people who do not truly see us, because we are unwilling to ruffle feathers or make others uncomfortable. But the only people
offended by your true self are the ones who benefit when who
you really are is hidden.

This book will challenge you to think differently about what
being yourself at work looks like. It will take you outside your
comfort zone and allow you to examine what authenticity really
means—and what it means to you. It will help you decide how
much of yourself you want to share at work, so you can take back
control of who you are.

The Real You

There is joy in finding the power of self.

There will be heartwarming hellos, laughs that fill your belly,
reintroductions that fill your heart. There will be days you look
in the mirror, proud that you get to come home to yourself, proud
to call yourself by your name, proud to stand firm on the things
you want for your life.

Stepping into your most authentic self is not without challenge. Learning to show up as the real you will come with hard
conversations—with yourself and others. Too often people love
the picture of you they have created in their minds, not the actual
person standing in front of them. There will be those who do
not accompany you on this part of your journey. There will be
those who refuse to see you no matter how vibrantly you show
up. There will be those who claim to love you when in reality
they love only the idea of you. There will be painful goodbyes,
and you will grieve them. And you will likely grieve the parts of
yourself that you let go because you used them as a shield.

I spent over two decades trying to cater to the happiness of others, dancing softly around the things about myself that made them uncomfortable. I put everyone's comfort ahead of my own. I valued how others perceived me more than how I perceived myself. But authenticity is not about how you show up for others. It's about how you show up for you. You are the tour guide in the journey that is your life. Make it worth exploring.

In his book *The Creative Act*, Grammy Award–winning producer Rick Ruben writes, "Expressing oneself in the world and creativity are the same. It may not be possible to know who you are without somehow expressing it." It is impossible to truly know who you are, at your most authentic, without leaving yourself the space to show up for you. The greatest expression of authenticity is honoring yourself for exactly who you are, the things you want, and the people you love—without shame and without doubting the power of your own voice.

As we navigate life, we will be asked to shrink or expand depending on the audience. I encourage you to make *yourself* your audience instead. Instead of trying to make everyone happy, make yourself happy. In a world that is begging you to be anyone but yourself, being exactly who you are is your strength.

Want more from Madison Butler on authenticity at work?
Watch this video:

Understanding the Authentic You

1

Getting Comfortable Being Yourself at Work

by Lan Nguyen Chaplin

I'm a business professor who has visible tattoos, seven earrings, and, on any given week, purple, blue, or pink hair. I come into work later than others and leave early to pick up my kids. I take Zoom calls in a hoodie in my backyard. During the past few years, there's been a lot of talk about what it means to be professional while presenting authentically. There's also been a lot of encouragement around bringing our full selves to our jobs. We're all aware of the benefits of being yourself at work: more life satisfaction, greater well-being, and higher levels of motivation, performance, and productivity.

Typically, though, being yourself while being taken seriously is easier said than done. This is especially true when you're just starting out in your career or when you're new to an organization. You haven't established your credibility, nor have you connected with those around you. You want to belong, but you don't know how. You're still trying to read the company culture.

I understand the dilemma. I haven't always felt so liberated in my appearance—more often, I've been a people pleaser. Out of fear of disappointing others or falling short of expectations, I've had a hard time setting boundaries around my personal and professional identities. It took me over a decade to blend the two in a way that I'm proud of and that represents who I am.

The best timeline for you in this respect is always going to be the one that feels right and safe. Don't feel pressured by the things you read online about why first impressions matter or why you have 90 days to establish your entire reputation. Authenticity is more about how you feel in this moment of your life and what you'll do to honor that identity.

Here's what I've learned throughout my journey—and what you can do to get more comfortable in your own.

Convince Yourself That You Belong in the Room

Whether you're just beginning your career or are changing roles, you're starting from scratch every time you meet new people. In these situations, you want to figure out which aspects of your background are exciting for you to spotlight and qualify you to be there. When you believe that you have something valuable to contribute, you'll feel more confident speaking and showing up authentically, and your fear of judgment will naturally dampen.

Why? Because you'll be focused on what really matters: using your unique knowledge and experience to make an impact. If you aren't convinced that you deserve to be in the room, how can you expect anyone else to be?

Here's how to get started.

Identify what you have to offer

Don't just have a general mantra of "I belong at the table." Take the time to create a thoughtful list of how and why you belong. Start paying attention to what makes you *you*—your background, talents, beliefs, and values. These are your strengths, and they will set you apart if you're willing to share them.

One question you can ask yourself: What is the organization missing when I'm not present? Write down your answers, including the results of the work you contribute. As you brainstorm, be clear with yourself about the advantage you and your skills bring to your team. If you're not contributing value, no one is interested in how passionate you are about your job or how late you log off every night.

For example, maybe you recognize that your experience as a multicultural and multilingual first-generation professional is your secret sauce. Because of your background, you are uniquely qualified to help your organization honor its public-facing commitments to diversity, and your input offers a competitive advantage to teams trying to tap into international markets. Maybe you're the go-to person for things that allow your team to run efficiently: the reliable colleague who always replies with thoughtful feedback, the peer who can easily weave together polarizing ideas, or the rising leader who isn't afraid to ask "Why?"

Don't make the mistake of thinking the things that come naturally to you are easy, and therefore unimportant, skills. Consider that your expertise is likely part of why you were hired; it's one of many things that your organization needs to drive value. And don't assume that coming straight out of college means you don't have enough experience to contribute. You can bring a fresh viewpoint to new and old problems, and ask questions that pin-point issues your more seasoned colleagues haven't considered or are less able to see.

Demonstrate gravitas

In the room itself, you need to have the confidence and credibility to capture the attention of your peers or seniors and create interest in what you have to say. When you can command an audience with your presence, people will take your voice seriously and want to know more.

Gravitas combines authenticity and clarity. For instance, when you speak up in a meeting, be clear about where your idea comes from, why it's important to you, what it offers the business, and what hard evidence supports it. On a deeper level, empathize with those who ask you questions, and try to view your colleagues as humans to connect with, not people to conduct transactions with. This mindset will help you come across as outwardly authentic.

> ➤ **PRO TIP:** Once you know what you offer, schedule informal coffee chats or lunches with influential people throughout the company who you hold in high esteem. Seek out people who are open-minded and who have shown you, or others, allyship and support. In my experience, this is a good way to become known to peers and superiors and to make your ideas and contributions visible. The more relationships you develop, the more welcome you'll feel.

Find Your Voice (and Be Vulnerable)

While you may want to appear faultless to gain the respect of others (especially as the new person), your imperfections are ultimately what will draw people in. You need to be vulnerable to build meaningful relationships at work, but finding your style—your unique way of expressing your humanness—is going to take some trial and error.

As an example, when I started my career as a professor, I met with a colleague who was loved by his students. We'll call him Jensen. I wanted to know how he did it. He told me that he connects with students by cracking jokes. That was his secret sauce, and I wanted to emulate it. The problem was, I tend to be more "serious" than "funny."

Jensen was a brilliant, charismatic, and witty academic with 20 years of experience. I, on the other hand, was just a few years older than (or the same age as) my students, and I was too nervous to feel anything except my heart racing when I stepped into the lecture hall. How would I ever succeed?

It took me a while to realize that what humor did for Jensen, compassion did for me.

Similarly, it's going to take you time to figure out how to express your vulnerability at the right time to the right people. Once you do, though, it can be a great way to make connections and build a foundation of trust that will make you feel more comfortable showing up authentically at work.

To begin, I recommend starting small.

Share something low-stakes with a team member

Choose someone you'd like to build a more meaningful work relationship with, and make it personal. For example, tell them a story about your weekend or a hobby you're getting into. Listen and look for cues on how they respond. Is their reaction positive? Are they willing to share something in exchange? Does the conversation make you feel positive and energized? If so, the relationship has potential.

The key here is learning how to read a room, as well as yourself. Through several small interactions you'll learn to better understand your audience, your own comfort level, and how you and others react to different types of information.

Consider the context

This includes the who, what, when, where, and why of the situation. Before sharing something more personal or higher-stakes with a coworker, consider the intention behind your words. I've shared stories about forgetting to pick up my kids at school, being mistaken for the caterer at a meeting with top leaders, and being a no-show on Zoom calls because I was operating in the wrong time zone. My intention was never to share some brilliant insight or life lesson. It was to humanize myself in front of an audience that saw me as a role model.

So consider the details of the situation: Are you looking for support? Are you aiming to build a friendship? Are you trying to tell a funny story that will make your colleague laugh, and in turn build a stronger connection between the two of you? Are you trying to relate to the other person with compassion? Have their reactions made you feel safe in the past? Do they tend to ask others about their personal interests and families? Do they talk about their personal interests and family? Do you trust this person? What feels natural for you to share?

Taking a moment to reflect before sharing will help you see the outcomes you want and avoid opening up to people who make you feel uncomfortable or don't appreciate your vulnerability.

> **PRO TIP:** Being vulnerable is letting your guard down just enough to allow others to feel human along with you. Your intention should be to build trust and to help your audience feel inspired. Don't be afraid to experiment a bit, draw inspiration from others, and figure out which kinds of vulnerability feel good and which don't.

Set Boundaries to Avoid Oversharing

Acting in ways that reflect your honest beliefs, emotions, and values may be one of the strongest predictors of well-being. At the same time, it's important to recognize that there is a certain time, place, and audience required for you to safely share those parts of yourself. It's possible to be yourself at work even if you don't publicly disclose every single thought or emotion to your team members. In fact, it's healthy to have boundaries and it's natural to want to keep some things private. So don't mistake vulnerability for oversharing. You won't be any closer to being authentic than the person who says nothing at all.

Your boundaries are based on your unique needs and wants. They are rules, created by you, that indicate what you will accept and what you will not, including how you want to be treated by others and show up at work. What and how much you feel comfortable sharing varies from person to person.

To figure out what's right for you, use this two-step exercise.

On a piece of paper, create two columns

On one side, write down your values and needs that must never be violated or compromised—your nonnegotiables. On the other side, write down the things that bring you happiness but aren't an immediate priority. You may, for example, want to establish a better work-life balance but be willing to compromise on or work toward that goal over time—making it a negotiable. Feeling safe enough to share your racial, sexual, or gender identity, however, may be a nonnegotiable.

As you fill out your columns, you may find that some of your answers are nuanced. For instance, inclusion (being able to share your identity or present authentically) may be a nonnegotiable, and privacy (having the autonomy to decide when and with whom you share) may be as well.

Write a personal philosophy

Are there any patterns in the thoughts, words, ideas, and actions you wrote down? Use these to come up with a short list of core values (e.g., inclusion, family, morality, integrity) and write down why they are important to you, how you practice them, and how they influence your goals. (We'll go more into defining your values in the next chapter.)

Now, use what you've written to come up with a short personal philosophy or a motto that feels undeniably true to you. My personal philosophy is, "I'm not for everyone and not everyone is for me. I choose to live a life with integrity." In moments of self-consciousness, small or large, I come back to it to remind myself of who I am and check my integrity. If I'm living my truth, then I let the panic go. My philosophy acts as a guide for my words and behaviors, and helps me recognize when a boundary needs to be set or has been crossed.

Your philosophy can similarly help you enter the workplace with confidence and recover when you feel your integrity or sense of self is being challenged.

> **PRO TIP:** Sometimes you may share something that you wish you hadn't. Give yourself some grace. It's going to take a little trial and error to figure out your boundaries, as well as other people's. In all situations, listen to your instincts. The sooner you and your colleagues can establish what behaviors you find OK versus not OK, the sooner everyone will know where they stand. Feelings of hurt, confusion, and frustration can be minimized.

For example, if you gauge that a team member may be uncomfortable hearing about your personal life, or if you decide that you feel uncomfortable sharing, there are ways to be honest while protecting boundaries and privacy for both of you. In these cases, a simple and honest statement will let people know what you need without oversharing: "I'm having a

hard time with all the demands in my life, and I won't
be able to respond to emails after 5 p.m."

Practice Deep Listening

It's often tempting to say things and act in ways that you think
might make a good impression even if it camouflages the real
you. For instance, how many times have you tried to appear
agreeable during a meeting because it's what the boss wanted to
see? In these moments, I encourage you to pause and practice
listening instead of reacting. When you listen deeply, you allow
yourself to be silent. Silence allows you to declutter your thought
process, be present, reflect, and make an honest contribution to
whatever is being discussed.

You are helping yourself be more authentic by processing
the other person's words with an open mind, reading between the
lines, and appreciating body language, cadence, and tone to gain
a richer understanding of their words. Whether or not you agree
with those words, you're showing the speaker that they matter
and you're giving the person the time and space to be themselves.
A respectful coworker will reciprocate and empower you to communicate your authentic self as well.

To put this into action, prioritize the following.

Keep an open mind

Craft a couple of go-to questions that will help you listen with
interest, especially in high-stakes situations when you may feel

pressure to react or make an immediate contribution. For example, you might try, "Can you explain what you mean by X?" or "When would this not work, and why?" When the person speaking responds, listen intently. You can even write down notes to help you better digest and understand people's ideas, then follow up one-on-one. This practice can help you develop the confidence to speak your truth, connect with others on a deeper level, and decrease any feelings of isolation you may be going through as the new person.

Create a time and space for important conversations

During private meetings with colleagues, put away your phone, listen, and observe nonverbal cues like posture, eye contact, and facial expressions. Aim to understand the other person's emotions about the topic. The simple act of being present will ground you and give you the time and space to process what you're hearing and react more authentically.

➤ **PRO TIP:** Deep listening is a skill that takes time to develop, but the more you do it, the better you'll get. As you practice, try repeating the other person's words back to them before you respond ("This is what I'm hearing from you . . ."). It will make them feel seen and heard while giving you extra time to process their perspective. Similarly, rather than planning a response while the other person is speaking, buy yourself time by asking for clarification ("What did you mean by X?").

. . .

Becoming true to yourself is a lifelong journey, one that will evolve and change over time as you learn more about your character and core values. My biggest piece of advice is to give yourself the gift of self-acceptance and cheer for others. The right people will reciprocate. When you can bring your whole self to work, you have a real chance to thrive and flourish.

QUICK RECAP

Being yourself at work is easier said than done. Here are some ways to get more comfortable showing up authentically:

- **Create a list of how and why you belong.** Pay attention to what makes you *you*—your background, talents, beliefs, and values.

- **Find your voice.** Consider the intention behind your words. You'll be able to see the outcomes you want and avoid opening up to those who make you feel uncomfortable.

- **Set boundaries to avoid oversharing.** You can be yourself even if you don't disclose every thought or emotion.

- **Practice deep listening.** Use the silence to declutter your thought process, be present, reflect, and make an honest contribution.

Adapted from "How to Get Comfortable 'Being Yourself' at Work," on hbr.org, July 13, 2022.

2

How to Find, Define, and Use Your Values

by Irina Cozma

What are your values?

As a career coach, when I ask my clients this question, I usually get one of two answers. They either say, "I've never actually thought about that" or "Oh, easy. These are my values . . ." After more conversations, the first group often realizes that they do have some ideas about their values, and the second group realizes that their values are mostly just a list of words without substance.

Both reactions are valid—it's not easy to have clarity around your values. After all, the importance of identifying and using them isn't emphasized in our society. Most of us aren't taught how to do this type of self-reflection in school. You likely won't be asked to identify your values for any job. And your employer will probably never base your annual performance reviews on them.

That doesn't mean finding, defining, and knowing how to use your values isn't important. There is so much power in understanding what your values are—they can help you make decisions, guide your career, and even live a happier life. The following steps can guide you through thinking about your values in an intentional way.

Step 1: Find Your Values

Your values aren't hiding. Even if you haven't articulated them, they're a reflection of the most important aspects of your life. Here's how to pull those ideas to the forefront.

Reflect on what's important to you

"Values" is just a label we use for the things that are important to us. Ask yourself: What do I care about the most in the world? Make a list with as many things as you can think of. Your list should reflect what is important and personal to you, not what others (family, friends, peers) may expect from you.

Honesty is critical at this stage. Try to sum up your ideas in as few words as possible. (You'll expand and further define your values later.) Some examples may include:

- Family

- Money

- Comfort

- Friends

- Career

- Time

- Freedom

- Optimism

Review the list and pick your top three values

You're probably thinking, *But they're all important!* While that might be true, some values are certainly more important to you than others. Again, honesty is key. If you're struggling to select three, you can choose two or four values instead. The number isn't important—the intent here is to keep the list as short as possible.

Rank your values

Once you have your top values, reflect on whether they have equal meaning to you or if you're able to rank them. There is no right or wrong approach here, but your answer should tell you something about how important these different elements are in your life.

This isn't a one-time exercise. You might need a couple of weeks or months to stabilize your top values. Take the time to reflect and revise. When I did this exercise myself, it took me almost a year to find and stabilize my values. Gradually, I realized that happiness and fairness are essential to me. Later I added freedom, which was so engrained in me that I could not identify it as quickly as the others. Pay attention to values that may emerge or become important to you over time.

Step 2: Define Your Values

Now that you know your values, it's time to define what they really mean to you in your own words. While you can look for the dictionary definitions of your values, the answers probably won't be there. It's important to come up with your own.

For example, with my value of freedom, there are many ways to define it. Here is how I define it versus how one of my clients defines it:

- *Me:* The ability to do whatever I want, whenever I want, and however I want it. This applies at the macro level (e.g., travel) and micro level (e.g., mental freedom).

- *My client:* I want to have independence in my actions and decision-making and not be micromanaged.

Same value, but two very different definitions.

At first, you may be tempted to write long paragraphs for each of your values to justify or explain them. But try to keep your definitions as short as possible—you want to be able to easily remember your values and how you define them. One succinct sentence will do. A test you can use to see if you're on the right track is to ask yourself: If somebody were to wake me in the middle of the night and ask me to define my values, could I answer?

As you work to define your values, don't be discouraged by the broad nature of the words or let others influence your perspective on what they mean to you. When I declare that "happiness" is one of my values, sometimes people roll their eyes. "That's an empty word," they'll say, or "That's too general." But for me, this word has a crystal-clear definition: Happiness is the joy found in the process of what you are doing.

Big words, but precise and personal definitions.

Step 3: Use Your Values

You'll know you have identified your values and truly defined them once you find yourself looking at the world around you through the framework of those values.

This is where you'll really start to see the power of knowing your values: They simplify decisions and actions. They can give you courage when you think you don't have it. They can guide you and provide you with valuable insights.

Here are some examples of values in action:

- If one of your values is fairness, this can guide you when you need to give constructive feedback to a colleague or a direct report. It wouldn't be fair to avoid confrontation when you know the feedback would be helpful to them. Fairness is being honest with them and giving them a chance to improve or remedy the given situation.

- If one of your values is optimism, you can better approach challenging situations with a glass-half-full attitude. Did you not get the job? That's fine—you got to practice interviewing and make some new connections. Are you overwhelmed by a busy schedule? You'll be OK—look at how much you're learning from these new experiences.

- If one of your values is family, that can help you make decisions regarding your career or where you'd like to live. If you get offered a job that would allow you to move closer to your parents, you can feel excited in taking it over another one based across the country. If you're wondering whether you should quit a position that has poor work-life balance, you can start looking for a new one confidently, knowing it would give you more time to spend with your loved ones.

At first, it might be challenging for you to connect your daily experiences to your values, especially as they evolve and solidify over time. One way to practice using your values is to reflect on a situation that's frustrating you. Ask yourself: What is lurking behind my frustration? Is one of my values not being met? Another way you can practice is by reflecting on situations that bring you joy. Which of your values is being fulfilled by that activity?

Don't expect to get clear on your values in one day. It will take time. Depending on your journey, your values might stay constant over time or they might change based on new events and information. Check in with yourself annually to make sure you're still in touch with the things that are most important to you. And remember: This exercise will help only if you're 100% honest with yourself.

When will you know if you have deeply held values? When you're unwilling to compromise on them.

QUICK RECAP

Your values can help you make decisions, guide your career, and even live a happier life. Here are three steps to identify and think about your values in an intentional way:

- **Find your values.** Reflect on what's important to you, then create a list of your top three values. Rank them if you can.

- **Define your values.** Write down what each of the values you identified means to you. Keep your definition as short as possible.

- **Use your values.** Begin to look at the world around you through the framework of your values.

Adapted from content posted on hbr.org, February 7, 2023.

Communicating Authentically, Without Oversharing

3

Using Authentic Conversation to Connect with Others

by Susan McPherson

You've probably heard this advice before: "Bring your authentic self to work." It makes sense. Being yourself is the best way to form meaningful relationships, which are integral to career success and growth no matter what field you work in. Research shows that people with a robust social network have better job performance, feel more fulfilled, and even live longer.[1]

But how do you actually share your authentic self in a professional setting, and how can you do it in a smart and sustainable way?

Showing up totally unfiltered and trusting everyone who crosses your path could go downhill quickly. On the other hand, if you keep things at the surface level and hide your true self, you might miss out on forming the types of relationships that can enrich your life and career.

As a business owner, this is territory I've had to navigate time and again—and I can tell you firsthand that building strong connections with my colleagues and peers is what has fueled my success. Here's what I've learned along the way about how to form these kinds of relationships in ways that feel productive and not draining.

There Is No "Work Self"

Do you feel like there's one version of you that shows up at work and another, more authentic version that shows up with friends? It's understandable—you don't choose your colleagues or clients, and most meetings require a certain degree of professionalism. But if you see networking and work interactions as transactional, you're likely missing out on an opportunity to form deeper connections, which can happen only when you show up as your full self.

Let me give you an example. I recently joined a business Zoom call where everyone was talking about the weather. "Oh, it's sunny there? It's so gloomy here!" Weather is not a bad topic; it's something we all experience. But it's also probably not going to lead to a meaningful conversation. When I joined the call, I related the weather back to something more personal: "I am not fond of rainy days because walking is *the* thing that helped me get through the pandemic. I've walked more than 1,200 miles in the last few months."

I shared something specific and vulnerable. I also spoke like a human, as I would in a room of friends. This isn't something I have to "try" to do—at least not anymore. It's a skill I've developed over the course of my career through regular practice. I learned that people become more comfortable when you show a wee bit more vulnerability. It's why, today, I don't have a delineation between work and personal connections: Friends I meet at the gym often turn into clients, and clients turn into friends who come to dinner parties.

I recommend you practice this yourself. Try to see everyone you come across as a human, rather than a work contact.

It's a Practice

Showing up as your authentic self is the baseline of building meaningful relationships at work, but it requires time and intent. The best tool you have here is *listening*. When I have a conversation with someone new and sense a good connection, I try to pay attention to important details like what they're passionate about, where they work, or something they've found specifically challenging.

Then, I follow up.

If I find an article that reminds me of our conversation, I send it. If I'm hosting an event that they might find valuable, I invite them. If I meet someone else I think they should meet, I introduce them. On a new business call, if I visited a restaurant recommended by a colleague, I make a point to let them know how good the hummus or pasta puttanesca was. Being an active listener also helps you quickly gauge who you want to build deeper connections with (or not).

What this all really boils down to, in addition to being a good listener, is asking, "How can I help?" Being generous with your suggestions, ideas, and connections—even when you don't need something from the other person—is one of the most powerful ways to connect.

That said, help in ways that energize you rather than exhaust you. Don't take on things that will require too much of your time—a three-minute introduction is low effort, but high impact!—and focus on helping people you authentically respect, rather than those who may take advantage of you or put you in an uncomfortable position.

You Don't Have to Connect with Everyone

Bringing your true self to work means being vulnerable, and not everyone deserves or needs to see that side of you. And you aren't obligated to help every person who crosses your path. Setting boundaries is important for a number of reasons: It helps you preserve your time, prevents burnout, protects you from breaches of trust, and allows you to focus on the relationships that give you joy.

Remember that the goal is not to tell your life story to every person the moment you meet them. You can build toward mean-ingful relationships with the right people—listen to your gut on whom to trust. Beware of people who only want to hear about you but don't reveal anything about themselves, or people who only want to talk and don't care to listen.

Relationships should be reciprocal. Choose a handful of people in your professional life who you want to deepen your relation-ships with, and ask them for a coffee date or a virtual drink. If you don't authentically enjoy the relationship, it's not worth your time.

. . .

Focusing on and making space for these deeper connections has allowed me to fuse my life and my work without burnout, overwhelm, or anxiety. It can work for you, too. You have the power to create your own communities. Begin with something simple: showing up.

QUICK RECAP

How do you share your authentic self with others in a professional setting, and how can you do it in a smart and sustainable way? Use these suggestions:

- **See everyone as a human, rather than a work contact.** Once you shift your mindset, you'll start building deeper connections.

- **Nurture your relationships.** Listen and pay attention to other people's interests and passions, and follow up when you come across things that remind you of them.

- **Set boundaries.** Bringing your true self to work means being vulnerable, but not everyone deserves to see that side of you. Put your energy into the relationships that energize you.

Adapted from "How Much of Your 'Authentic Self' Should You Really Bring to Work?," on hbr.org, February 12, 2021.

4

My Pronouns Are They/ Them. What Are Yours?

An interview with Lily Zheng by Paige Cohen

Two years ago, I attended a Christmas party at my parents' house in California. Picture a dimly lit room filled with candles, wine, cheery tunes, and garlands twinkling in the background. I was standing in the kitchen, picking cheese from a platter, when a relative resembling a Disney villain pronounced that I looked more masculine than she remembered. She sipped her drink and cocked her head to the side, taking in my buzzed hair, green vest, and slacks.

"You were a very feminine child," she said. "You wore little bows and dresses." She reached her manicured claw toward my plate and snatched a chunk of cheddar.

It had been a long time since I lacked the language to explain my own identity, but there I was, at a loss. The room spiraled in on itself and once again I was a budding teen, standing in front of a mirror, trying and failing to verbalize what was happening in my mind and to my body. The difference was that, in my actual teen years, words like genderqueer and nonbinary were unknown to me. My experience was hard to articulate—to myself and to others—because I didn't have the vocabulary to name it. The gender norms I observed as a kid, which were reiterated in my home and in the media throughout my adolescence and young adulthood, made it difficult to imagine any other way of being.

But now, I was educated. I had created a life for myself in Boston. I wore a suit one day and slathered my eyes in compostable glitter the next. My friends never asked questions. They cheered in celebration.

So why did I stare blankly at my relative and say nothing?

While her words were rude and probably transphobic, they forced me to turn inward in a way I hadn't in years. When I did, I came to a realization: Even with the privileges and safety my queer community provides me, this interaction was difficult because it hit on something deeply tied to who I am. Clothes and haircuts may not mean everything to everyone, but for me, they are tools that allow me to share myself authentically with other people. My presentation signals how I feel inside—not entirely like a "she," not entirely like a "he," but somewhere in between. Nonbinary.

To have another person recognize that part of me, and then openly ridicule it, was very painful.

It would be nice to live in a world where people like me, or any member of the LGBTQIA+ community, never have to justify our existence. Some people actually do live in that world. But for those of us who fall outside the fine lines of what is considered mainstream, lacking the language to name and explain our experiences is still dangerous.

I use the pronouns they/them/theirs. Like the clothing we all use to express our genders, pronouns are labels that make us more visible and indicate we are not alone. I think about what it would have meant to my younger self had I discovered this sooner. It's the kind of progress that can save lives.

Even so, I'm navigating the implications of my decision: How do I share my pronouns with other people? How do I ask other people what their pronouns are? How do I figure all of this out, especially in professional environments?

I talked to Lily Zheng, coauthor of *Gender Ambiguity in the Workplace*, to get a little guidance.

Paige Cohen: *What's the best way to share your pronouns, both in life and at work?*

Lily Zheng: Be clear, straightforward, and casual—the same way you'd share what region or city you live in. In person, share them with your basic intro: "Hey! My name is Lily Zheng. I use they/them pronouns, and I'm a diversity, equity, and inclusion strategist living on Muwekma Ohlone land in the San Francisco Bay Area."

If you don't have the chance for a formal introduction, you can shorten it. "Hey! I'm Lily, they/them pronouns. You?"

Online and in email signatures, you can include your pronouns, typically in the format of X/X or X/X/X (e.g., she/her or she/her/hers), somewhere easy to see.

Is the process different when you're first meeting people versus when your pronouns change after having known someone for a while? For example, if your colleagues are used to using she/her or he/him pronouns for you, and you now identify with they/them pronouns, how do you let them know? Do you owe them an explanation?

I had this experience myself. After using she/her pronouns for my entire young adulthood and professional career, I started using both they/them and she/her pronouns mid-2020, and moved fully to they/them pronouns by the end of the year.

Beyond changing the pronouns on my social media and online bios, I was casual but firm with folks about the changes as I was making them. First, I told people, "I'm using both they/them and she/her these days! No worries about using they/them all the time, but I'd very much appreciate the effort."

Later I said, "I'm using just they/them now. Thanks for understanding and respecting that."

You owe them as much explanation as if you were describing your move to a new city—that is, only as much as you feel enthusiastic about sharing.

I'm a little scared that when I tell someone my pronouns they are going to want to have big conversations around them. I don't always have the energy for that, and other times it feels too personal. How do you navigate that kind of situation when it comes up?

Remember that you have a huge amount of leeway over how to talk about your pronouns—your *discursive framing*, if you want to be fancy about it.

If you speak about your pronouns in a hushed, apologetic voice, you are positioning them as a topic that you don't expect people to understand. If you speak about them in a defiant voice, you are positioning the topic as one you expect to receive resistance and conflict on. If you speak about them as casually as you're talking about what you had for lunch, you're positioning them as a nonstarter when it comes to discussion. You have the agency to decide which framing to use in any conversation, given your relationship with the person, the context of the situation, and your own capacity and energy levels.

If you've done that and somebody still pushes your boundaries with their inquiry, you can gently but decisively enforce your boundary with a statement and/or humor that indicates the question was inappropriate.

Let's say a colleague asks you this: "But *why* they/them? Isn't that controversial? Does that mean you do drag?"

You might just redirect them: "We're in the middle of a meeting about this product, and I'd like to stay on topic—email me later this week and I'll be happy to chat then."

Or you could add some humor in your response: "Ha, you want my social security number while we're at it? I'll send you a resource to learn more if you're curious."

What should you do if someone calls you by the wrong pronoun?

Give a simple but clear correction, without apology.

> Colleague: "This is Paige. She works on the editorial team."
>
> You: "Oh—I use they/them pronouns. Thanks!"

What should you do if you call someone the wrong pronoun?

Give a simple apology and immediately make the correction by restating the sentence where you misgendered the individual.

> Colleague: "Oh—I use they/them pronouns. Thanks!"
>
> You: "My mistake, sorry. They work on the editorial team."

Don't over-apologize, attempt to explain or make an excuse for why you may have made the error, or passive-aggressively make the correction. Apologize, make the correction, and move on. Importantly, update your mental understanding of the individual so that the correct pronoun comes to mind the next time you interact.

On the other end of this, are there best practices for how to ask someone what their pronouns are?

Asking about pronouns can be complicated. On the one hand, not asking can lead to potentially incorrect assumptions and misgendering. However, in practice most people don't ask everyone their pronouns—they tend to ask only visibly transgender or gender-nonconforming people. In my experience, that can be marginalizing and insulting, especially when someone singles me out in a crowd to ask my pronouns.

My advice is to focus instead on always introducing yourself with your pronouns. If the person you meet feels comfortable doing so, they may share their pronouns with you. For all people who have not shared their pronouns with you, commit to using singular "they" until you learn their pronouns.

Should cisgender people share their pronouns?

That's an easy yes: All cisgender people should share their pronouns. In the same way that men in the workplace making use of flexible time or parental leave normalizes when women and people of other genders do so as well, cisgender people who share their pronouns (not with a "savior" mindset but simply as a matter of course) normalize the behavior when trans and gender-nonconforming people do the same.

Where allies can go wrong is when they make an overly big deal or show out of sharing their pronouns. That has the opposite effect of casting the action as strange or unusual, and makes it *more* difficult for trans and gender-nonconforming people to do the same without repercussions.

If someone tells you that they take more than one pronoun, like she/her and they/them, how do you navigate which you should use?

If people share that they use multiple sets of pronouns, make your best effort to use the different sets they've shared. If you feel comfortable, you can ask them whether they prefer people to switch between the different pronouns within the same conversation (e.g., "I was talking to her the other day. They told me . . .") or alternate pronoun sets in different conversations (e.g., In one conversation, "I was talking to her the other day. She told me . . ." and then in another, "They mentioned that to me before! They were saying . . .").

Resist the urge to *only* address them by the pronoun set that feels most comfortable for you, even if it's a set that they have indicated they are OK with.

QUICK RECAP

What's the best way to tell someone your pronouns? Be clear, straightforward, and casual. Here are some tips:

- In person, share them with your basic intro: "Hey! My name is Lily Zheng. I use they/them pronouns."

- Online, including in email signatures, you can include your pronouns (typically in the format of X/X or X/X/X).

- Rather than asking others for their pronouns, focus on always introducing yourself with yours. If the other person feels comfortable doing so, they may share their pronouns with you.

- For those who haven't shared their pronouns with you, use singular "they" until you learn their pronouns.

Adapted from "My Pronouns Are She/They. What Are Yours?," on hbr.org, June 15, 2021.

To see an illustrated version of this piece, follow this link:

5

Self-Disclosure at Work

An interview with Katherine W. Phillips
by Amanda Kersey

Self-disclosure is a key element of authenticity at work, but finding a balance with it can be difficult. What is OK to share? How much? To whom? And how do you share personal details without *oversharing*?

In the following conversation, I talk to Katherine W. Phillips, who, before her death in 2020, was a professor of leadership and ethics at Columbia Business School. We discuss why sharing information about our personal lives helps us build professional relationships and why individuals from underrepresented groups might hesitate to open up to their colleagues.

Amanda Kersey: *What does research say about self-disclosure in the workplace?*

Katherine W. Phillips: I've been doing research on diversity and inclusion in teams for the last 20-plus years. One of the major findings in the literature is that diverse groups tend to be less cohesive than homogeneous ones. I started thinking about that and took two or three steps back to think about how teams actually become cohesive. What is cohesion? And how do you build it?

As I started having conversations about that with some colleagues, we began looking at the literature and realized that a lot of cohesion is relationship. It's connection, trust. It's building real relationships with the people that you work with. And that requires some self-disclosure. You have to share things about yourself.

I had some personal experiences that drove me to think about that. I thought about how uncomfortable I sometimes was sharing personal details with colleagues that I worked with every day, that I thought I trusted, and that I thought I had great relationships with. I found myself censoring some of the information I was willing to share. That gave me the insight I needed to understand a little bit more about how to build relationships across boundaries in the workplace, because it's going to be critical for helping those diverse teams reach their potential.

You have a story about when one of your colleagues asked you what you did over the weekend. Could you share it?

This story actually started this research stream. I was having a birthday and was very excited about it. It was a Friday, so I had the whole weekend to celebrate. Everybody knew that it was my birthday.

When I showed up at work on Monday, all happy-go-lucky, one of my colleagues asked, "How was your birthday? What did you do this weekend? How did it go?" I said, "I got together with some really good friends of mine that I hadn't seen in years. We went out to dinner, and we went to a concert." He responded, "Oh, a concert. Who did you see?" And I said, "You wouldn't know him." Then I focused again on dinner and the great restaurant.

I kind of swept under the rug who I had gone to see, and it bothered me for a while. Why didn't I want to share with him that I had gone to see Kirk Franklin, a very popular African American gospel artist? Somehow I felt like my colleague wouldn't know who this person was, and maybe it would highlight that I'm Black. Maybe it would highlight that I'm a Christian. I just felt like those were things that perhaps I shouldn't share with him.

But as I thought about it, I realized my colleague never would have hesitated to share with me. He's told me about all these groups he's seen that I've never heard of, and I'd say, "OK, cool, good for you." I never judge him because of the music that he likes and listens to. It was an *aha* moment. If I don't embrace who I am, if I don't love who I am, if I don't share who I am, how can I expect other people to do the same?

How does being in the minority, whether it's due to race or sexuality or politics, come into play with authenticity and self-disclosure?

When we started this research, we wrote a paper called "Getting Closer at the Company Party." Part of the idea behind the paper was that companies have events—activities, happy hours, Christmas parties, etc.—that they ask all employees to come to with the expectation that it will somehow bring people closer together and create better relationships. When we did this research, we asked people, "Do you go to these events? Who's there with you?

How similar are they to you? How close do you feel to them after the party's over? And you do see some positive uptick, especially when people share the same identity?"

When people are in the minority, or they're very different from the people around them, they don't get that same uptick of positive feelings of closeness with people after they've engaged in these things. They were basically telling us, "I go to these events because I have to." They're not really feeling like it's going to lead to something different for them. That was true for anybody who felt that they were surrounded by people who weren't like them, even if they were part of what we might consider a majority group in the United States.

But then we did some research with African Americans specifically to ask them, "How comfortable would you feel sharing with or talking to people who look different from you in the workplace?" We got evidence time and time again that people were more comfortable with others who look like them and that they were concerned that sharing something about themselves that was different would create more distance between them and others, as opposed to bringing them closer. They were concerned that sharing might have negative implications for their credibility and their status in the workplace.

So it is a real concern. When I've written about this, I've used stories from executives on Wall Street who say, "Look, my numbers were perfect—they were better than anybody else's—but I still wasn't getting the promotion. And when I talked to my boss about what was going on, they said, 'We don't know you.'" It was important for those people to make a decision about how much they wanted to connect with others in the workplace. It can have big implications.

You have another story, when you had to take a risk on what you were going to tell your colleagues.

Yeah, this story is another *aha* moment for me, and definitely a risk that I had to decide if I wanted to take or not.

I'm from Chicago, born and raised, and when this story happened I was on the faculty at Northwestern University. My parents were still living on the South Side of Chicago with my very large extended family. I was at work, and I got a call from one my nieces saying, "You need to get down here to the South Side right away, because Mom and Dad have been arrested."

I was frazzled—I was like, *I've got to go.* I had to leave very quickly.

Of course, when I came back to work, my colleagues asked, "What happened? Is everything OK? Is everybody OK?" I had to decide if I was going to share with my colleagues that my parents had been arrested because the police chased one of my nephews into the bathroom of my parents' house. Who knows if he had done anything wrong. Things unfolded from there.

I decided to share it, mostly because there was no good alternative in my opinion. The consequence of me saying, "This is too difficult to share with you," lying about it, or saying, "Oh, it was nothing" wouldn't be better than just telling the truth. So I said, "This was a very difficult situation. And I want to share with you all what happened."

They were super supportive. They asked again and again how things were going. Because of going to court and other stuff, it was a year and a half before everything was over with. I think it was really a bonding moment. It gave my colleagues an opportunity to see that although I had made it—here I was, a professor at Northwestern—as an African American woman I was dealing with a life that they didn't see, and that actually gave them more respect for me.

It seems like sometimes self-disclosure is something we can choose to do. We can choose to share information, and that can be strategic when trying to build relationships at work. But sometimes it happens by surprise. There might be a family emergency, or someone might ask you a question that you weren't expecting to get.

It's a very common experience. The reality is we're all on our own journeys of identity and are deciding how comfortable we are disclosing various things about ourselves. For me, my racial identity is very visible. It's not something that I've ever thought about hiding.

But I certainly have been in contexts where I might want to be careful about how much I highlight it, or how much I let it take center stage. It's very normal for people to want to belong. We all have a need for belonging, and we often have concerns that if we highlight things that are different about us, that might make us feel like we don't belong where we are. It's absolutely normal.

QUICK RECAP

People often worry that sharing something about their personal lives, especially if they're in the minority, might have negative implications for their credibility and status at work. Consider these points as you decide what and when to share:

- Sharing personal information helps build cohesion and trust in professional relationships. Without it, you can miss out on career opportunities.

- If you're tempted to keep something to yourself, remember that if you don't embrace and share who you are, you can't expect others to do the same.

- If you're not comfortable in a certain context, you may want to be more careful about what you share.

Adapted from "Self-Disclosure at Work (and Behind the Mic)," *Women at Work* podcast, season 2, episode 11, November 26, 2018.

To hear Katherine W. Phillips's full interview, listen to this podcast:

Should You Disclose an Invisible Marginalized Identity at Work?

by Dannie Lynn Fountain

When I was a freshman in college, I worked overnights as a shift manager at the local McDonald's. One night, my team members in the prep line were talking about their love lives. A colleague made a comment about their friend who happened to be in a queer relationship. The response was universal: disgust. I had yet to come out to my peers and was left in the uncomfortable position of leading a group of people who found me repulsive. I was terrified. What if my girlfriend popped in for lunch? What if my classmates saw me at the register and mentioned my personal life? Despite my positional power, I felt unsafe.

In this moment, and in countless ones since, a silent part of my identity was either judged or accepted without anyone recognizing that someone in a marginalized community was present. I am a queer, multiethnic, neurodivergent, heavily tattooed, married, plus-size, first-generation-American, cisgender woman. I was raised in a lower-class household and currently am a debt-free member of the upper class. With the exception of my tattoos, gender identity, and body size, every identity listed here is invisible in my presentation.

An *invisible marginalized identity* is any identity that is frequently marginalized and can be invisible in our daily presentation. My biracial identity is marginalized, but because I present as a white woman, it is invisible. Similarly, my sexuality, neurodivergence, and other identities are frequently marginalized but are not immediately evident when you meet me. Finally, there are aspects of my identity that are visible and are also stigmatized by society, such as weight. For most of my professional life, for example, I've presented as an "overweight" person, encountering uncomfortable instances of navigating office chairs that I couldn't fit into, silent judgments about foods I ate, and, often, listening to conversations about health and diet at the office lunch table. Now, after losing 180 pounds, I no longer present as overweight, but I'm still considered "morbidly obese" according to the medical standard of the body mass index.

When parts of your identity are marginalized and invisible to others, moving through the world can feel a bit like walking around with dynamite in your pocket. You know it's there—the weight of it reminds you of its power—and any unsuspecting passersby could spark an explosion. It's a frightening position to be in, especially at work. Sometimes the invisibility is accompanied by silent relief, but most times it's lonely. While fatphobia, for instance, is still very much a part of my day-to-day life, it no longer impacts my career advancement like it used to. In other cases, split-second decisions about whether to respond to microaggressions at work take up more headspace than any other part of my job.

The questions in my mind are circling and exhausting: How much of myself do I reveal to my colleagues? What parts do I hide? What should I consider before making those choices? How can others accommodate or accept the identities they refuse to acknowledge or can't even see? Based on my personal experience, here's what I've learned.

When Should I Disclose an Invisible Marginalized Identity at Work?

First and most importantly, there is no mandate to disclose any identity, ever. There is a reason that job applications include a voluntary self-identification form. Choosing to disclose a marginalized identity may result in new or additional stressors at work, none of which are your responsibility to bear—but they do impact your ability to earn an income.[1] There is absolutely zero shame in choosing *not* to disclose an invisible identity for the purpose of protecting your earning ability. Survival trumps disclosure, always.

In a climate of toxic and persistent microaggressions, however, keeping invisible marginalized identities hidden can be exhausting. Making the choice to disclose invisible identities can, in many cases, become the spark for change. Here are a few instances when disclosing a marginalized identity might be helpful:

- Preventing the marketing team from launching an offensive, or at the very least harmful, campaign or product. For example, sharing about your invisible mixed-race Latinx identity might help your team understand how a digital marketing campaign centered on "sugar skull makeup" for Halloween could be offensive and considered cultural appropriation.

- Helping internal company culture initiatives to be messaged through uplifting means. For instance, disclosing a personal story about fatphobia could dissuade the team from voting on a team name that would demonize fat people.

- Shaping the way we think about language at work. For example, talking about your personal experiences with mental health could be an inroad to explaining why replacing the words "crazy" or "insane" with more precise language might be helpful in conversations with others.

In each of these cases, the benefits of speaking up include making the workplace a healthier and more respectful place to be every day.

There is also the consideration of whether to disclose something during the hiring process versus once you're an employee. Overt or covert discrimination can occur during and after hiring despite legal protections, and seeking recourse can often involve a lengthy process. If you're marginalized but are not granted legal or political rights or recognition, the protections don't exist at all. For example, being part of the LGBTQIA+ community may not be legally recognized in some countries; neurodivergence isn't always protected under disability laws; and weight-based identities are unprotected in many U.S. states.

Disclosing during the interview process may help you gauge the employer's reaction to your disclosure, and understand whether you're likely to feel respected and included in your day-to-day work. After all, an interview is your chance to vet the employer and determine whether it will be a good fit for you. Ask questions that help you learn more about the company culture as well as managers' attitudes and beliefs around diversity and inclusion. In other words, disclosing in the interview may be the best option, as it'll help you get a truer picture of the employer's perspective while also opening up legal recourse if you experience discrimination after your disclosure.

How Should I Disclose an Invisible Marginalized Identity?

Making the decision to disclose an identity takes thoughtful consideration and a very serious weighing of the pros and cons. The psychological safety within a team, the potential support of a manager, and the overall company culture are all important factors. If you feel comfortable being vulnerable and honest with your colleagues, the next step is to determine how to share specific details.

Often, the action of disclosing an invisible marginalized identity takes place in stages. It may start with joining a company mailing list or an employee resource group. For me, the first disclosure of my neurodivergence at work happened by joining the ADHD, autism, and disability email lists at my company. These kinds of mailing lists may provide additional context and resources for how others have disclosed their identities, or templates

Disclosing Neurodivergence

by Ludmila N. Praslova

Every time I write about autism and neurodiversity, my inbox fills with notes from talented young professionals. I've heard from people who mask their autism to avoid stereotyping or discrimination at work. I've read painful recollections from employees who are shunned, bullied, exploited, or underpaid as a result of being neurodivergent. Then, there are those who were rejected or fired after disclosing autism, ADHD, or another neurodifference. Some of them want my advice. Others want to be heard. Their stories vary, but each resonates in some way. I myself am autistic.

People in the neurodiversity community are creative, funny, sensitive, empathetic, and accomplished. We help one another. But given our experiences in the workplace, it's no surprise that deciding whether, when, and how to disclose details about our identities is especially difficult. Some people hide their identities at work for many reasons, such as a fear of bias or bullying. Some may want to disclose early in the application process because they need specific accommodations—for example, many autistic people benefit from receiving interview questions in writing or having a quiet work environment. Others may want to get to know their colleagues and build some trust before disclosing. Whatever your decision is, it can come from a place of dignity and strength.

For instance, if you're in a job interview, you could be up front while also pointing out your strengths by saying something like: "I am sensitive to noise, but that also means I'm highly focused at work." If you wish to disclose without revealing your diagnosis, you can make your preferences clear in a subtler way: "I work better when I'm in a quiet space. It makes me more productive."

While some managers or coworkers could react to disclosure negatively, don't let that discourage you. When you own who you are, you may end up finding some allies or even inspire others to disclose their disability or identity.

Personally, I find disclosure both liberating and socially responsible. When we assimilate into systems that discriminate against us, we may unwittingly perpetuate discrimination. That said, don't pressure yourself. You might be a private person, your environment may not feel safe, or perhaps you just want to do more research. So, take your time, and if (or when) you feel prepared to talk about your identity, remember that your difference isn't a flaw. It's just that: a difference.

———

Adapted from "Autism Doesn't Hold People Back at Work. Discrimination Does," on hbr.org, December 13, 2021.

that can be leveraged for future disclosures. If another individual has shared about an identity that you also hold, they may have created an FAQ document to decrease the number of personal questions they had to navigate. You may be able to leverage this same document (or something similar) during your disclosure. (For more on the challenges behind sharing details about autism, ADHD, or other neuro-difference, see the sidebar, "Disclosing Neurodivergence.")

The next stage of your disclosure may be a one-on-one conversation with your manager. Ideally, this is a conversation where you share not only the identity in question but also the impact of that identity. For instance, does your neuro-divergence present alternative ways that you might prefer to receive feedback? Does your mixed-race identity make you uncomfortable on Taco Tuesdays due to the nature of team conversations or behavior? Anchoring a disclosure on how it impacts you and the team will help the manager decide what to do next.

The final stage of the initial disclosure might be choosing to share your identity with the broader team. It may happen immediately after the previous two actions, but it may also happen with a bit of a delay or when the opportunity arises in a team setting. This stage is the most variable, centering primarily on your comfort level and the context of team culture. You could start by confiding in one or two people and then slowly opening up to the rest. You might say, "Hi, I know we work together pretty frequently on X project. I wanted to share with you that I have ADHD, which causes me to struggle with Y. By sharing this with you, I'm hoping we can adjust to Z process to accommodate this."

Disclosure of an invisible marginalized identity is not a one-time decision. As you may have heard in the stories of those in the LGBTQIA+ community, "coming out" with an invisible identity is an ongoing process and may occur again and again with changes in role, team, responsibilities, company, and more. Be aware that the decision to disclose an invisible identity may differ in each of these contexts. That is, you may disclose your identity to your immediate team but not to ancillary department teams that you also work with semi-frequently.

At the end of the day, remember that you hold the power of disclosure and you have the context to know whether disclosing something will harm your workplace safety. The decision to disclose (or not) ultimately rests with you.

QUICK RECAP

Invisible marginalized identities generally aren't seen in our daily presentation. If you have an invisible marginalized identity, you can disclose it, but consider the following first:

- Only disclose if you feel comfortable and safe.

- In some situations, making the choice to disclose can be the spark to create change.

- When interviewing for a job, consider disclosing after you make it to an in-person interview.

- If you decide to disclose, find resources created by listservs or employee resource groups in your company.

- Have a one-on-one conversation with your manager. Discuss how your identity impacts you and the team, and how your boss can support you.

- Open up to colleagues or teammates as you feel comfortable doing so.

Adapted from content posted on hbr.org, January 25, 2023.

To learn more about neurodiversity at work,
listen to this podcast:

7

Coming Out as Trans at Work

by Michael Cherny, Shalene Gupta, and Sandra J. Sucher

I've known I was different since I was eight years old, but the process of coming out has been a journey of a thousand steps.

I joined Deloitte full-time in 2012. Shortly after that, I assumed a leadership position with the pride employee resource group. However, it wasn't until 2019 that I decided to come out publicly as trans after meeting my partner. Her unwavering support of my identity made me realize I wanted the world to embrace and see me as she did. I was already in the process of transitioning socially, but at the time, no one at work knew.

My partner gave me great advice. She asked me: What are you willing to sacrifice? Are you prepared to be an island? Are you prepared to lose your job, your friends, your family? And I realized I was.

I decided to come out on my birthday. I took a four-pronged approach. First, I scheduled one-on-one conversations with individuals I wanted to make sure I spoke to before I was out publicly.

Second, I went really broad and published an article on our internal website. Third, my leader at the time sent an email to the entire practice—about 900 people across Canada. Finally, I did the good millennial thing and posted on social media. I dressed up in a suit and tie—it was my first time wearing a tie to work—and my partner took a photo of me in the lobby wearing a button that said "Birthday Boy." I posted it on social media with the caption: "Hi, I'm Mike. And today is my first day living my truth."

I didn't expect the overwhelming response I got. People were texting me, calling me, and I had thousands of comments on Instagram, Facebook, and LinkedIn. To date, my LinkedIn post has received more than 500,000 views.[1] After countless speaking engagements, articles, and even a cover feature in a magazine, I've told my story to more than a million people.

I still get messages asking for advice about coming out at work, and I try to respond to each of them because I remember the feeling of not knowing where to start or who to turn to. I try to provide the support I wish I'd had, because coming out is complex. There is no playbook. There is no one right way to do it.

By coming out, I'd unwittingly become a trailblazer in the corporate world. I didn't have a choice about being a trailblazer, but the choice I do have is to be a road paver, someone who ensures the path is just a little bit easier for everyone else going through a coming-out journey.

As part of that effort, I've created a three-phase framework for thinking through what can happen before, during, and after coming out at work. Because everyone's experience is different, I turned to an incredible network of people to ensure this framework includes multiple perspectives:

- Rachel Clark, an information security specialist at TD Bank

- Ry Maisonneuve, an inclusion leader at Deloitte Canada

- Sophia David, a professional and leadership learning leader at Deloitte Consulting India

- Harrison Browne, an actor and former professional hockey player

- Maeve DuVally, a managing director of corporate communications at Goldman Sachs

- Owen Heighes, an assistant vice president at MetLife

- Katherine (Katie) Dudtschak, an executive vice president at RBC

Their wide variety of experiences and strategies speak to different cultures, contexts, and situations. There's no one right or wrong way to do this: Ultimately, it's about navigating the journey in a way that is true to yourself.

Before

Calculate your risks

When I came out, I was prepared to quit my job and have all of my social connections disintegrate. Thankfully, that didn't happen, but the tragic reality is that many places are transphobic and you may need a backup plan.

I also worried that I would be taken less seriously as a professional and passed over for promotions. Coming out actually gave me a platform and a way to connect with others more authentically, but again, I was lucky. That's not everyone's experience. So, think about what you are risking and what you are willing to give up.

Rachel Clark came out in 2007—20 years into a technology career that included C-suite roles—after quitting her job, and she had difficulty getting back into her industry because of discrimination. Doors she'd always thought would be open slammed shut. She was eventually able to find a job, and she's commented that today we live in a more progressive era. While we still have a long way to go, there's more dialogue now about what it means to come out and be trans at work, and more people are visibly and openly challenging stereotypes and misconceptions. She stresses, however, that if she could go back and do it all over again, she would have come out sooner.

Do your homework

Read up on the laws about discrimination in your country and city. Learn your company's policies on discrimination to find out how protected you are. Dig into the details of your company's policy on gendered spaces, such as washrooms, and the dress code if there is one. Identify the gaps. Assess how important these gaps are to you and if you are willing to advocate for policy changes.

Look up your health insurance policy, too. Is hormone therapy covered? Surgery? Mental health support?

Make a list of all the people you'll have to notify for a name change. Don't forget important documents such as identification (a passport or a driver's license), insurance policies, security badges, and email addresses.

Maeve DuVally did trial runs of her new routine before she transitioned at work. On weekends, she took the time to go to women's locker rooms and familiarize herself with the space and lock in her routine. "Going into the women's locker room was very intimidating to me given [the controversy around the 'bathroom bill'] in North Carolina," she said.[2]

Advocate for policy changes or protection if you need it

When Sophia David came out in 2019, it was a crime to be LGBTQ+ in India. However, after she successfully battled cancer, she realized that for her, coming out was necessary. Since Deloitte is an international firm, she reasoned that if there were no legal protections in India, she could advocate for Deloitte Consulting India to create a policy that protected her. She was in the unique position of working for the Deloitte U.S. offices in India, which means the offices are an extension of Deloitte's U.S. office.

Sophia went through an exhaustive process of meeting with leaders to ask for their support and introductions to other influential leaders. Once she had a crew of leaders backing her, she spoke with a sympathetic talent expert at Deloitte Consulting India who took action to create an inclusive policy and guidance to support LGBTQ+ employees that was comparable to what employees in the United States received. This included ensuring health insurance covered hormone replacement therapy and gender reconstruction surgery. Once the policy was published, Sophia began speaking with other members of her team as well as her managers about her identity, and subsequently sent a note out to the larger office.

With the support of her employer, Sophia finally felt comfortable taking a calculated risk to come out. However, someone's ability to self-advocate varies. And as Sophia points out, her position at Deloitte enabled her to advocate for herself in ways that not everyone has access to, and her desire to come out in an environment where it was illegal was out of necessity.

Figure out who you need to inform

I did a pulse check before officially coming out. Before I came out at work, I slowly came out to the people closest to me and figured out how they felt, what their reactions were, and how best to prepare for those reactions from others in the future. I started by writing down a list of about 25 people I wanted to tell personally, and systematically had one conversation after the other. It was tough. How do you start that conversation? I actually ended up writing out a script.

Owen Heighes started by going to his boss. Together with HR, they developed a strategy to identify people he wanted to connect with prior to updating his name and pronouns in the corporate directory. Owen has a highly visible, global role and chose to have one-on-one conversations with specific leaders at his company first. Maeve DuVally worked with a representative from HR to make lists of internal employees and external stake-holders who should be told in advance of the larger announcement, as well as to determine who the news would come from: an HR rep, Maeve, or her manager. Ry Maisonneuve eschewed a company announcement and simply added their pronouns to their LinkedIn profile; then, they branched out to their email signature and finally to introductions during meetings. Katherine (Katie) Dudtschak stressed that her company partnered with her exceptionally well; the firm clearly respected that this was her story and plan. She owned it and made the key decisions.

Rachel recommends preparing for the unexpected: "There were people I thought would be allies and people I thought would be absolute nightmares. I was 100% wrong."

During

Manage your mental health

The day I came out, I booked myself in back-to-back meetings so I wouldn't have to talk to anyone. It wasn't the wisest idea in retrospect. There was an overwhelming response, and even though it was positive, managing it took a lot of mental and emotional energy.

Give yourself the time and space to process all of these emotions. Lean on your personal networks for support. Don't be afraid to ask for time off or to seek out therapy. The transition is a big one, and it stands to reason that you'll have a lot of emotions that will take far more than one day to process.

Maeve had a similar experience—and was even shadowed by a *New York Times* journalist during the first three days of it. She says that over time, people got used to her new identity, accepted her, and moved on with their lives.

Katie took the opposite approach. She came out by video with her CEO and her boss, and then worked remotely for two months, during which she went through some medical treatments, spent critical time with family, and prepared for her new life. "I was so afraid that if I sensed any negative visceral reaction, it would ruin my self-confidence," she said. "So I chose to not be at the office, I chose to be away from the office, do conference calls. This also gave the company time to let the more than 20,000 employees of the division work through important transgender training."

Manage the people around you

At one point, I had a list of who knew and who didn't, which helped me stay organized. The most common reaction I got was, "I support you, but I don't know how to be helpful." After a while, it can be draining to become the go-to source for everyone's questions. I've been lucky to have some amazing people step up and say they'll help me with that.

I actually had a friend from Deloitte's pride employee resource group lead a closed session with senior members of the firm. She went over transitioning, explained what I was going through, and answered any questions—everything from the basics (like "What does transitioning actually mean?") to "How can we support Michael?" and "How do we answer questions on bathroom policy from other employees?" I didn't have to be there, and she debriefed with me afterward. Now I try to offer myself as a similar resource to people around the world when they need it.

Similarly, while Katie was out of the office for two months, her company held trainings so that she knew everyone would have time to process her transition and adjust to it. While she was away, Katie was flooded with hundreds of emails, each of which she took the time to respond to. This has continued to this day. "It was incredibly important to recharge emotionally and be ready to come back to work as me," she said.

At Goldman Sachs, Maeve's manager sent an internal memo to her floor the day she came out. She noted that in several ways, coming out actually strengthened her relationship with coworkers who are also underrepresented. "I was perceived to now belong in a group that might experience discrimination," she said. "I developed richer and more authentic experiences."

Owen notes that he was intentional about not correcting people publicly if they were making an honest mistake, like accidentally using the wrong pronouns in referring to him. "My goal was to normalize my transition, and correcting the mistake draws more attention to something," he said. "I gave it grace in the moment. A lot of people would make a mistake and apologize behind the scenes. I took it offline if it was important. I wanted to remove the feeling of walking on eggshells from the process." He stresses the importance of assuming positive intent and remembering it's a process for everyone, including yourself.

While it is important to assume positive intent, unfortunately people who harbor negative sentiments and perceptions about trans and nonbinary individuals do exist. If you do face bullying at work, make sure to refer back to the policies and protections you researched earlier or identify what recourse you have against discrimination. Don't hesitate to use these policies and mechanisms to report or respond to any harassment or workplace bullying. Lean on your allies in and outside of the workplace to both support and advocate for you, and recognize it is not your responsibility to educate or manage these individuals alone.

Manage physical and emotional changes

When I decided to come out, I was nervous about navigating the fact that I was going to change physically and emotionally. How do you begin a conversation about suddenly using a different washroom, wearing different clothing, or, in my case, growing facial hair and having a deeper voice?

I started from a place of honesty and vulnerability. None of us—me or the folks around me—had been down this road before. I talked to my leaders and walked them through what I was feeling and what I needed, whether that was time off, flexible hours, or the space to experiment with a new leadership style. I had to be very aware of my emotions to make sure they weren't impacting the people I managed. In addition, I was gracious and open about how affirming comments like "Love the facial hair" or "Is your voice getting deeper?" felt to me and how much I welcomed them. And most importantly, I leaned on my networks. I often asked my partner and friends for a sanity check on my emotions.

But that was just my approach. Owen notes that he chose to navigate the early stages of his transition privately until he was at a place where he was prepared to have conversations around his physical and emotional changes.

After

Coming out is a continual journey. You don't get to take it back once you're out. I've been out since 2019, but I still have to come out to people who don't know me. I routinely speak at diversity and inclusion events where I have to come out to clients who otherwise see me as a white cis-passing male. Sometimes my voice trembles when I say my name and my pronouns out loud, just like it did in the early days of coming out. It still feels surreal—and yet it's the way it's always been inside of my head.

There are still daily challenges. I deal with microaggressions, such as getting deadnamed (called by my former name) and misgendered, daily. It messes with my head, and I'll wonder, *Did I do a good enough job of being me today?*, which is an outlandish question. I haven't figured out all the answers, but I try to take it one day at a time and ask for support when I need it.

Manage the spotlight

When I came out, I was suddenly thrust into the spotlight. In many ways this has been positive: I've been able to speak and connect with people I otherwise wouldn't get to meet. However, it wasn't an experience I was necessarily prepared for. "Once you come out, people are going to demand your emotional capital," Rachel notes.

A former professional hockey player, Harrison Browne is no stranger to the spotlight, but he struggled to balance being a role model for the trans community with taking care of his mental health. "I needed to distance myself from some of the news for my mental health," he said. "As a result, I wasn't as prepared as I would have liked to be for a panel, and I had to forgive myself for that."

Maeve recommends thinking strategically about which engagements you want to speak at to avoid burnout. She suggests picking awareness days such as Pride Month and Trans Awareness Week, since these are moments when the greater community is paying more attention to trans and nonbinary experiences.

Owen stresses that you don't have to be a spokesperson. "You don't have to lean into all the forums and be the person representing," he said. "I don't represent all trans people. I represent my own journey."

Establish boundaries

When you're in the spotlight, it can be easy to feel that you owe the public everything about yourself. It's important to establish boundaries. Owen recalls that someone once told him, "People have to earn the opportunity to ask specific questions." He uses this advice as a touchstone to decide what questions he answers and from whom. There are people he's happy to have a long, in-depth phone call with and others he'll simply point to resources. He's careful about which details he shares publicly and which are purely personal.

"I've been very open about my story. But there's no reason that everybody has to be as open as I was," Maeve notes. "If there are certain aspects of your story that you don't want to go public with, that's your right. It's your life. It's your story. It's your story to tell. And you can tell it in any way that you want, because it's your story."

Recognize the void

One aspect of coming out that I was wholly unprepared for was the void I felt afterward. I'd prepared for weeks, months, and years for this big moment. Then I did it. I was living my truth. I felt grateful, drained, and ready for the rest of my life.

And then I hit the void. The adrenaline rush was over. My networks weren't checking in as much. I wondered what I was supposed to be doing next. The world saw me as living my truth, affirmed, and validated, but it didn't see how hard it can be to suddenly be thrust into the spotlight while still maintaining the same level of performance at work. Not only that, but now you're hyperaware of the people around you, braced for being deadnamed or other microaggressions around your gender and name.

It's particularly important to stay connected to your networks during this time and to continue taking care of yourself emotionally and mentally. "Avoiding the void after means not letting the airwaves get too quiet," Katie said. "Recognize you're not a burden and ask for check-ins. It's easy to perceive silence as 'something is wrong' or as a rejection, but in reality, people see you're OK on the outside and want to leave you alone to exist."

For me, coming out was a gift. It freed up what felt like 40% of my brain that was constantly thinking about my identity, wondering whether or not I should come out and what would happen if I did. I've been enormously lucky with the loving and supportive response I've received from my personal and professional networks. While there are still challenging days, coming out has helped me relate better to other people and created a platform for me to share my journey and help others be themselves, while also supporting organizations to become more inclusive workplaces for everyone.

There's no cookie-cutter approach to coming out as trans at work, but my hope is to help create a world where the path will be paved with more than just good intentions—with building blocks that make the journey a little bit easier for everyone else walking down this road.

QUICK RECAP

There is no one right way to come out at work, but here are some tips for managing the process:

- **Before:** Calculate the risks, do your homework about laws and company policies, and advocate for any policy changes or protections if you need to. Then figure out who you need to inform.

- **During:** Monitor your mental health throughout the process. Manage the people around you in a way that feels comfortable but not draining, especially when navigating physical and emotional changes.

- **After:** Take control of the spotlight you're in; you don't have to be a spokesperson. Remember to establish boundaries with others, but stay connected to your network.

Adapted from content posted on hbr.org, October 12, 2021
(product #H06MBP).

Want to know how to support someone coming out as nonbinary
at work? Read this article:

Dealing with Real Emotions

8

Managing the Hidden Stress of Emotional Labor

by Susan David

With the possible exception of *Sesame Street*'s Oscar the Grouch, very few of us have the luxury of being completely and utterly ourselves all the time at work. The rest of us are called upon to perform what psychologists call *emotional labor*—the effort it takes to keep your professional game face on when what you're doing does not align with how you feel. We do this outside the office too (making polite chitchat in the elevator when you're feeling tired and surly comes to mind), but it is perhaps more important at work because most of us are there many hours per week, and our professional images and livelihoods depend on how we come across.

Say, for example, your boss makes a meant-to-be-inspiring comment about doing more with less, and you smile and nod, but what you'd like to do is upend the conference table. Or a customer talks down to you about the poor service she says she received, and you're unfailingly polite and solicitous even though you resent being patronized. Or perhaps you simply had a bad night's sleep, yet you push yourself to remain energetic and upbeat because you've been told—more times than you care to count—that "great" leaders bring positivity and inspiration to their teams.

Emotional labor is a near universal part of every job, and of life; often it's just called being polite. But how one *acts* makes a meaningful difference. A person can *deep act* in a way that is still connected to their core values and beliefs at work ("Yes, the customer is being patronizing, but I empathize with her and care about solving her problem") or *surface act* by faking or suppressing their emotions ("I'll be nice here, but deep down I'm really spitting nails").

Research shows that the tendency to engage in this latter aspect of emotional labor—surface acting, in which there is a high level of incongruity between what people feel and what they show—comes with real costs to the person and the organization. When people habitually feel the stress of surface acting, they're more prone to depression, anxiety, decreased job performance, and burnout. This has an effect on others, too: Leaders who surface act at work are more likely to be abusive to their employees by belittling them and invading their privacy, for example. And job stress can spill over into home life. In one study of hotel employees who did a lot of surface acting on the job ("Yes, sir, I'd be delighted to bring you a fluffier robe!"), their spouses were more likely to see their work as a source of conflict, and to wish their partners would find another job in the hopes that their relationship would be less strained.[1]

There are common contexts in which surface acting comes about, including:

- A mismatch between your personality (for example, level of introversion or extroversion) and what is expected from you in your role

- A misalignment of values, when what you're being asked to do doesn't accord with what you believe in

- A workplace culture in which particular ways of expressing emotion (what psychologists call *display rules*) are endorsed—or not

The ideal, of course, would be to work in a job to which you are so well suited that your actions and feelings are always in perfect harmony, eliminating the need for you to be exhaustingly inauthentic all day. In real life, however, the goal of keeping your surface acting to a minimum and instead engaging in deep acting, where the role is aligned with who you truly are, is a more attainable one. Assuming you find meaning in the work you do and don't feel you're in the entirely wrong field, here are some ways to reduce your emotional labor and feel better about how you're spending your days.

Remind Yourself Why You're in the Job

Connecting to your larger purpose will help you feel more connected to your work. For example, maybe you're learning skills that are critical to your overall career, or you're in a dull but stable job right now because you need money to support your family.

Explore "Want to" Thinking

It's easy to fall into the mentality that work is something you "have to" do. And most of us don't have the financial resources for work to be optional. But allowing yourself to appreciate the aspects of your job that give you a charge—maybe it's brainstorming with colleagues or making systems more efficient—elevates your work into something you choose to do, rather than something required of you. To be clear, I am not suggesting you "just think positive" or try to rationalize away real concerns. But do become more aware of the subtle traps of language in which work tasks, even ones you might enjoy, are framed as chores. If you can't find a true "want to" in key components of your work, it may be a sign that change is in order.

Do Some Job Crafting

Consider whether you can work with your manager to tweak your job so that it is more aligned with what you value. For example, when you visit different offices of your firm, if you're stimulated by the new people you meet and their unique ways of doing things, perhaps you could propose a project that involves more of these kinds of visits. The goal is to make your job more interesting so that less emotional labor is required.

When we typically think of stress at work, we focus on time pressures, information overload, and change as the causes. Yet the emotional labor that you invest in your job can be a significant source of demand, and it's worth considering and managing.

QUICK RECAP

We've all experienced emotional labor at work, the effort it takes to keep a professional face on when what you're doing does not align with how you feel. Here are some steps you can take to reduce your emotional labor and feel better about how you're spending your days:

- Remind yourself why you're in the job you're in by connecting it to a larger purpose.

- Stop thinking of work as something you "have to" do. Reframe it as something you *want* to do.

- Use job crafting to tweak your job so that it is more aligned with your values.

Adapted from content posted on hbr.org, September 8, 2016
(product #H034C1).

To hear more from Susan David on emotions at work,
listen to this podcast:

9

Do You Ever Second-Guess Yourself?

by Tucci Ivowi

Once I was in a large auditorium filled with marketing and sales professionals who were gathered to attend a training program on the fundamentals of the coffee business. I was a brand manager in a company I had just joined. During the training, someone asked, "What's the difference between soluble coffee and roast and ground coffee?"

It was a simple question. I knew the answer. But I still refrained from raising my hand. What if it was a trick? What if I was wrong? What if I wound up looking foolish?

It was my first day on the job as a new recruit. *It's probably best for someone with more experience to respond*, I thought to myself. I didn't say anything and someone else used the opportunity to speak up.

Turns out, I had the right answer.

This wasn't a one-off scenario. There have been so many times throughout my career when I've second-guessed my abilities. You know the feeling—that nagging voice in the back of your head, clouding your mind with doubt and insecurity.

Imposter syndrome.

I finally told myself: *You know the answers. You're smart. You have to say something.* I came to realize that even if my answer *was* incorrect, I would learn something new. The benefit of speaking up outweighed the emotional cost of my silence. I looked at the evidence and it showed me that no one in my organization had been penalized for getting something wrong. In fact, they had been rewarded for their participation.

After that, I made it a point to contribute. I began to share my point of view, whether or not it differed from the majority perspective. People began to notice. They said I had "leadership potential."

Years later, I joined the senior leadership team of a multinational organization. I was working out of Ghana and heading a business unit for the Central and West African region. At the age of 36, I was the youngest and first African woman to have held that role. I was also the first woman on an otherwise all-male team. Exhilarating as it was, stepping into my new position meant that a number of employees—both men and women—looked up to me as a source of inspiration for what I had achieved and the odds I had beat.

I was already nervous to take on a more senior role, but those feelings were compounded by another truth: I was representing a group of people whose own careers may be helped or hindered by my success or failure.

My imposter syndrome snuck back in. I wondered, *Am I the right person for this job?* So I reminded myself that I was there because I was capable. I had to continue doing what I had done throughout my career: Focus on the job, give it 100%, and deliver results. Nothing more and nothing less.

If you've recently been promoted or found the job of your dreams but feel yourself being overtaken by imposter syndrome, I understand. There is probably a myriad of questions going through your head:

- How did I get here?

- Am I really good enough to be doing this?

- Can I handle these responsibilities?

- Will I make a fool of myself?

- Will my former colleagues think I'm undeserving of my promotion?

Based on my own experiences, here are five pieces of advice that can help you dial down the self-criticism and grow in your career while remaining true to yourself.

Acknowledge That It's Normal to Feel Nervous

Imposter syndrome is particularly common when you're new or a minority among a group of people whose appearance, behavior, or experiences differ from yours. It's normal to feel uncomfortable. Remember that you won't be in the minority of newcomers forever. Someone else will be hired or promoted at one point or another and join the ranks. Suddenly, you'll be one of the old hands, and a part of your role will be to help the new person settle in.

In the meantime, a certain level of nervousness and doubt is good. It counterbalances complacency and can push you to work harder. When I shift my perspective in this way, it helps me get out of my mind and look ahead. Acknowledging your feelings, but also understanding that they are common, has a way of calming your senses by reducing the angst and reminding you to focus on your goal.

Don't Harbor a Fear of Failing

Here's one thing I've learned: The best people can fail, and the most unlikely people can succeed. The unlikely ones are those who fall, get up, and try again and again until they finally reach their goal.

Push your fear aside and focus your nervous energy on learning and adding value to your new role. Take it one day at a time. When you identify an area of weakness, own it. Think of it as an opportunity to grow. This is how the best leaders gain confidence.

I have always taken personal growth seriously, but I rarely wait around for my organization to send me to workshops or training programs. Most times, the best lessons can be learned at home or on the job.

I read a lot about my areas of business and spend time studying case studies relevant to my work. If you feel you don't have enough information on your industry, read up. If you need to get better in a particular area, ask your employer if they'd be willing to invest in sending you to a course. If you want to improve your presentation or communication skills, practice first in front of family members who can give you honest yet loving feedback, and then in front of colleagues who can give you more technical tips.

That said, if you do have the resources, setting aside time to invest in your career development—both at and outside of work—can be incredibly valuable when it comes to getting ahead and beating the odds.

Doing this work will grow your confidence—but don't wait until you're perfect to put it into practice. Real learning requires trying and sometimes failing along the way. As ironic as it may sound, failure is one way of refining your craft. You learn everything that can go wrong, and you find solutions to do it better the next time.

Be Sincere with Yourself and Others

A big part of imposter syndrome is feeling that you don't belong. But if you are clear about who you are and what you stand for, you are less likely to try to fit into a mold that wasn't designed for you in the first place. It's only after you are able to own who you authentically are that you can forge your unique path forward and become the kind of leader others want to follow. Being insincere with yourself is a trait that will lose you both supporters and respect.

Reflect on what makes you tick, what makes you comfortable or uncomfortable, and what values you stand for. For example, you might realize that you're normally reserved and subdued in large meetings but are more comfortable stating your opinions in smaller groups. Think about how you can still contribute in larger settings without feeling intimidated. Or start small: Practice being your authentic self in low-risk environments until you're more confident, and then it will come naturally to you.

Remember, You Don't Have to Have All the Answers

You'd be hard-pressed to find someone who is skilled at everything. If you've been promoted, it means someone in a position of power recognizes that you have certain skills, and those skills are important to succeed in the role they are trying to fill. Like everyone, you are better at some things than others. You have strengths and weaknesses. It's useful to be aware of your weaknesses so that you can improve and grow. But you should also capitalize on your strengths. Those strengths are what got you to where you are today.

For example, if you're a people person, use that skill to increase your influence on your new team. If you have strong project management skills, volunteer to facilitate meetings. In those meetings, contribute to the topics in which you have expertise. Remember that you're in the room because of your unique expertise, just as others are in the room because of what they offer. Your goal is to work together as a group to reach your organization's missions or goal. This can't be done by just one person. No one person has all the answers.

Find an Ally

If you're still feeling like an imposter after practicing these tips, find an ally or a group of allies to be your support system. My allies have always come in the form of peer coaches: organic, mutually trusting relationships with peers I'm comfortable taking feedback from because I trust that they have my best interests at heart. Some organizations have a peer-coach program that matches individuals with one another. If your organization does not, there are other ways to form these relationships.

Ask someone whom you respect and get along with, and hopefully they will accept. It can be a simple ask: "I really appreciate your insights. Since I'm just starting out, it would be great if I could lean on your guidance and get feedback on how you think I'm doing in this role. Would you be my peer coach? I am happy to reciprocate if that would help you, too."

The benefit of having a peer coach within your company is they see you firsthand at work every day. They observe your behaviors, witness your contributions, and can give you unbiased, independent feedback. They can point out your strengths (which will, again, do wonders for boosting your confidence) and advise you on areas for improvement.

For example, one of my pet peeves is people who talk in meetings just to be heard, even when they have nothing new to contribute. I tend to add my voice to the conversation only if I feel I have an additional point to make. My peer coach observed this behavior and told me to speak up more in meetings because my contributions were considered cogent by the group. They reminded me that when I offer my voice, I can influence decisions.

Their words have helped me grow from a person who didn't feel comfortable asking or answering questions in meetings to someone who comes to the room with solutions to problems.

Everyone needs support, even leaders. They are smart enough to know they can't do it alone. So don't be afraid to ask for help.

. . .

A certain level of self-doubt is good because it pushes us to work harder. But own your strengths so that you see what everyone else sees: that you are not an imposter. You were hired or promoted for a reason, not merely out of the kindness of someone's heart. You are there because you have shown what you can do. You are there because you're an asset.

QUICK RECAP

Some self-doubt can be good—it can push you to work harder. But when it manifests as imposter syndrome, it can backfire. If you've recently been promoted or found the job of your dreams but are feeling like a fraud, the following tips can help:

- Acknowledge that it is normal to feel nervous.

- Focus your nervous energy on learning and adding value to your new role.

- Be sincere with yourself and others about who you are and what you stand for.

- Capitalize on your strengths.

- Find an ally or a group of allies to be your support system.

Adapted from content posted on hbr.org, July 28, 2021.

For more on imposter syndrome, watch this video:

10

Your Job and Your Identity Are Two Different Things

by Tim O'Brien

Jake is three and he is tired. He wants to be picked up and held. "It's OK, sweetie," his mom, Kate, sings as she reaches down to pick him up. Midway through the lift Jake writhes, throws his head back, and knees her in the stomach. Kate knows she should not take this breakdown personally. Most days she knows that mom gets kicked sometimes; it is part of the job.

But when Kate takes a kick at work—when her report is criticized in a meeting, for example—she does take it personally. It is harder for her to remember the difference between "Kate" and the role she fills as a "senior analyst." And when you take professional kicks personally, you compromise your ability to recover and see the bigger picture. You fail to read the kicks as symptoms of a bigger organizational dynamic or challenge.

Your formal organizational role is an important anchor: It grounds you in your task and helps you know how to relate to

Are You Too Emotionally Invested in Your Job?

by Melody Wilding

How can you tell if you're too emotionally invested in your work? Look for these signs that it's time to pull back:

You take criticism personally. When someone criticizes your work, it can feel like a confirmation of your worst fears—that you're not good enough. Before you jump to conclusions, separate criticism of your work as a *product* from criticism of you as a *person*.

Work follows you home. You may work more to feel good about yourself or struggle to turn off at the end of the day. You're not proving your dedication

others and to the organization. But when you bring most of yourself to your job—your experience, training, abilities, knowledge, effort, quirks, and passions—you feel as though you are more than just your role. This is especially true when you are always on and never quite leave work behind. You can quickly forget you are filling a role in order to accomplish a task on behalf of an organization's or a group's purpose. You cannot reflect dispassionately on organizational challenges, seeing your work and role as one piece of a larger puzzle. Instead of maintaining a bird's-eye view of the system you are in, you place yourself at the center by always being on—rather, you're undermining your success.

You're a people-pleaser. You have a tendency to put others' needs ahead of your own, whether it's fixing situations or changing your opinions in an attempt to keep the peace. You're not being helpful if it comes at the expense of your mental health and the quality of your relationships.

Your identity is your job title. If you don't have any self-concept beyond what you do for a living, that's a precarious place to be. A little psychological distance from your work can go a long way to boosting your well-being.

———

Adapted from content posted on hbr.org,
December 8, 2022 (product #H07DOK).

of what looks like "your" problem in a workplace drama. This weakens your judgment and makes it even more likely that you'll take criticisms and decisions personally. The pattern worsens when you conflate your role with self-worth, thinking you are only as valuable and useful as the position you formally fill. (Unsure if your identity is overly tied to work? See the sidebar, "Are You Too Emotionally Invested in Your Job?")

It is critical that we learn to distinguish and differentiate our *roles* from our *selves*. We get into trouble when we lose ourselves in our jobs instead of thinking in a detached way about how the jobs are viewed by others. It can be very rewarding to throw all our education, training, talent, and passion into our work, but we forget that others in our organizations are reacting to the role we represent in *their* work lives, not necessarily the interesting and thoughtful people we think we are. Here I will share some of the insights I've gathered in my courses at Harvard Kennedy School, where I try to help students disentangle themselves from their roles so that they can be better leaders and make the differences they want to make.

The role you fill belongs to your organization, institution, group, or family. Other role-holders have expectations of you in that role, and those expectations may be reasonable (that you perform your tasks well) or unreasonable (that you speak on behalf of all women, represent your minority group, or always be the person who takes meeting minutes). Meeting those formal expectations and managing the informal ones is essential to retaining your job. Your job may also come with conflicting expectations from different authorizers, such as your boss or clients—never mind the multiple roles you fill at any given time, each with their own set of authorizers. Balancing all this is a dynamic process that must be actively managed. Chances are, when you lose your perspective on your different roles, you're misreading the organizational dynamics.

Kate, a composite of people I've counseled, shared two instances when she lost sight of the difference between her role and her self—lapses that left her feeling bruised. The problem was that Kate overidentified with her role, and when others had trouble dealing with her in her formal role, she took their responses too personally.

Consider: As an analyst, Kate worked hard to organize complex sales data in a way that her colleagues could quickly understand. To do the job right, analysts must sometimes share unpleasant information; disappointing colleagues is inevitable. When Kate's colleagues didn't like her findings, they often pushed back and questioned her methodology. Their resistance left Kate feeling angry and insecure.

She needed to remind herself that her colleagues' rejection had everything to do with her *role* and nothing to do with her personally. When teams were confronted with their poor results, they felt embarrassed, got defensive, and scapegoated the analyst and her work. Their feedback to Kate said more about them than it did about Kate. But that was hard for her to see when she couldn't distinguish herself from her role.

When Kate was promoted to director and her peers became her direct reports, her social interactions at work changed dramatically. She was left off an invite for a team happy hour, and colleagues who used to be friendly became guarded. These changing dynamics are a reminder that people relate to you through the role you have in their lives. When Kate's position changed, the role she played in her colleagues' work lives also changed and they struggled with how to relate to Kate the director. Kate herself struggled as she took these shifting relationships personally, resenting her colleagues for primarily reacting to her role and not maintaining their warm and candid relationships.

Kate did not know how to be a boss and a friend at the same time. At first, she doubled down on the friend role, insisting to her colleagues that nothing had changed. But as she developed a new appreciation for the challenges of management, it was harder for her to sit by as her team complained about their bosses. As much as she wanted to be part of the group, the relationship was different. Her role as director meant the team needed her to guide them. Again, Kate felt kicked and bruised as she and her colleagues wrestled with how to relate to each other.

Once Kate embraced the responsibilities of the role and the inevitable authority dynamics that come with it, she was able (through much reflection) to draw the line between that role and her self. Identifying *less* with her role allowed her to live into the role *more* fully and happily. She was able to achieve a level of resilience that enabled her to perform well at work while maintaining a healthy sense of self.

QUICK RECAP

When you can't distinguish between your role and your self, you can take setbacks at work personally. Doing so can compromise your ability to recover and see the bigger picture. Consider this advice:

- When you get negative feedback at work, remember that it is about the work, not you.

- Embrace the responsibilities of your role and the dynamics that come with it, which can help you better draw the line between your role and your self.

- Identifying *less* with your role can increase your resilience and help you perform well at work while maintaining a healthy sense of self.

Adapted from "When Your Job Is Your Identity, Professional Failure Hurts More," on hbr.org, June 18, 2019 (product #H050HO).

11

So, You Cried at Work

by Melody Wilding

"Are you OK?" a stranger asked as she tapped me on the shoulder outside my company's office in Manhattan. I looked up at her with wet, red cheeks and wiped tears from my eyes.

Minutes before, I was in a team meeting when my boss made a derogatory comment, minimizing my professional background and training. His remark broke me—it was the last straw on top of my already overwhelming workload. Though I wanted to push back and assert myself in the meeting, my voice cracked and a lump formed in my throat. Fighting back the waterworks, I could only mutter, "Excuse me," as I rushed out the door and out of the view of my coworkers.

At the time, I felt profound regret and shame about my reaction. What I didn't realize is that I was part of the 45% of professionals who have cried at work.[1] I also count myself among the 20% of people who are highly sensitive, meaning I think and feel everything deeply. Decades of research proves that sensitivity isn't a character weakness.[2] Rather, the trait is associated with greater processing in brain areas related to emotion, self-awareness, and vividness of experiences.

Maybe you also have shed a tear in the office, perhaps when your performance review didn't go as planned or when you received bad news about a friend or family member. While we typically associate crying with loss and grief, it can be a reaction to anger as well. Many people cry when they feel frustrated, anxious, or deeply passionate about and invested in their work.

Over the last year, many of my coaching clients have asked how to recover from crying at work. It's no surprise, because workers are under greater stress and facing record rates of burnout. As a result, emotions—and the likelihood of tears—are running high, even when teams are distributed. The new version of crying in the bathroom has become turning off your video to regain your composure.

If you have ever cried at work, then you know it can feel embarrassing. You may worry about what your colleagues think of you or how your outburst may jeopardize your professional standing (especially if you're a woman). What can you do to minimize the impact of crying at work and ensure it doesn't hurt your reputation? Here's how to bounce back with strength and professionalism.

Reframe the Impact

Crying at work is not career-ending. Research shows that others are generally more empathetic than you might imagine. A survey of over 2,000 senior executives found that 44% of C-suite leaders believe crying is OK from time to time, and another 30% believe it has no negative effect on how you are perceived at work.[3]

With these facts in mind, extend yourself compassion. Refrain from harsh self-criticism and judgments that will only worsen your pain. Instead, reassure yourself that one moment doesn't define you and that difficulties are a part of life. Remind yourself that emotions are not only normal and expected in the workplace, but when leveraged correctly, they can be a super-power. While crying at work may not have been your proudest moment, your emotions have a flip side: They serve as a positive source of making better decisions and empathizing with others.

Give Yourself Space

You won't be at your best if you're emotionally hijacked. So when the waterworks set in, ask to pause the conversation. Take five minutes to compose yourself. For example, step out of the room or turn your camera off. A quick change of scenery and a few deep breaths do wonders for quickly diffusing heightened emotional reactions.

Studies find that leaders who engage in situation modification, which involves changing your external environment to lessen the impact of your emotions, are the most successful at regulating their reactions.[4] Recognizing your need for space and diplomatically requesting it signals self-management and emotional intelligence—two indispensable leadership qualities that account for 90% of what sets high performers apart.[5]

Address Crying Courageously

Your first instinct may be to apologize for being "overly emotional" or making others uncomfortable. Avoid this, as it puts you
in a disadvantaged position. Not only are you making potentially
false interpretations, but you're also diminishing yourself. Stay
away from pushing your emotions down and trying to pretend
as if they are not there. As I often say, what you resist persists—
the longer you try to fight an emotion, the more powerful it
becomes.

Instead, respond from a place of strength. Acknowledge your
reaction rather than trying to hide it. You can say something like,
"As you can see, I am very invested in the success of this project,
which is why I'm having an emotional reaction." Employees who
attribute their tears to passion are viewed as more competent and
promotable.[6]

Focus on Follow-Up

The *recency effect* suggests that our most recent behavior is recalled
best. So if you want to preserve or recover your reputation after
crying at work, focus on creating a positive impression in your
very next interaction. Keep your reply solution-focused and
forward-looking. For example, you could say:

- I really value our working relationship and want to make
  the project successful. When can we regroup and come to
  an agreement about how we'll move forward?

- Thank you for providing me with feedback today.
  I appreciate everything you shared and am working on
  action steps to implement what we discussed.

- I had a strong reaction today because I'm overwhelmed by changing priorities at the firm. I'd
  like to review my workload with you and determine
  what can be delegated or eliminated for the time
  being.

Likewise, go the extra mile on your next deliverable. Deliver-
ing above and beyond the expected standard shows you're resil-
ient, capable, and committed.

Have a Plan for Next Time

Crying often happens as a result of being caught off guard and
not knowing how to process your feelings in the moment. This
is especially true if you're a highly sensitive person. Arm yourself
with strategies to channel your emotions before they get the better of you.

You can access calm without shedding a tear by control-
ling your breathing. Before, after, or during a stressful encounter, you can try box breathing, a method used by Navy SEALs.
Or keep an ice-cold glass of water nearby. Drink up as you
feel tears coming on to lower your body temperature (and
your fear response) and get rid of the lump at the back of your
throat, called the glottis. You can also put your angst into a
small item in your hand, such as a stress ball, a medallion, or
a pen.

Seek More Help If You Need It

Crying at work once in a while is not abnormal. But if you regularly find yourself weepy at the office, it could be wise to seek out the support of a therapist. Involve the appropriate parties if your tears are the result of bullying or other mistreatment. Take time to evaluate whether you're in a work environment that will best support your growth and mental well-being.

Remember, it's human to have emotions. What makes you a great leader is how you choose to respond and communicate when those emotional reactions do arise. If you take ownership of your feelings and reactions, it conveys strength and confidence that others will respect.

QUICK RECAP

Crying at work can feel embarrassing. You may worry about what your colleagues think of you or how your outburst may jeopardize your professional standing. Here's how you can minimize the impact of crying at work and bounce back with strength and professionalism:

- Reframe the impact and extend yourself compassion.

- Take some space to compose yourself.

- Acknowledge your reaction instead of hiding it.

- Create a positive impression in your next interaction.

- Have a plan for next time.

- Seek more help if you need it.

Adapted from content posted on hbr.org, January 4, 2022
(product #H06RPR).

How much emotion is too much emotion at work?
Listen to this podcast to learn more:

When Identity and Work Collide

When You Don't Feel Comfortable Being Yourself at Work

by Dorie Clark

Sometimes the corporate cultures in which we find ourselves don't match our personalities. Occasionally, that can lead to healthy creative friction; other times it creates painful pressure to conform. That was the situation facing one of my executive MBA students. "I'm having a problem at work," she told me. "I keep getting feedback that I'm distant, and I think it's harming my career." The reason she was getting that response, she admitted, is because she *was* acting aloof. "I'm not sure how to be my real self at work," she said.

Many of us face similar problems. In her case, she was a free-spirited Burning Man devotee who found herself working for a buttoned-down corporation. The pressure runs the other way, too: In an episode of the podcast *Startup*, a Gimlet Media staffer admitted that he felt out of place as a regular churchgoer amid his liberal, secular colleagues in Brooklyn.

In some instances, it pays to keep your opinions to yourself; it's probably best not to engage a coworker whom you know to be your ideological opposite in a conversation about a presidential election. But when it comes to your fundamental identity rather than your opinions, hiding or downplaying things can actually be detrimental to your career in the long run. As Sylvia Ann Hewlett and Karen Sumberg's research has shown, out LGBT workers are more successful than their closeted counterparts, likely because they don't have the added stress of managing their identities on top of the work they're expected to perform.[1] And Deloitte research shows that covering, or playing down differences at work, also has deleterious psychological consequences.[2]

So how do you know when it's safe to be your authentic self at work? As an openly gay consultant who has worked with more than 100 clients over the past decade, from *Fortune* 500 companies to government agencies and international NGOs, I've identified four questions that are useful to ask yourself.

What's Your Evidence for Believing You'll Be Penalized?

Have you actually seen others receive professional punishment for being themselves? We might believe we know how a certain action or disclosure would be received, but it's important to remember that unless you've seen direct evidence, it's only conjecture. That grizzled, macho supervisor maybe actually be a PFLAG member with a gay brother. And even if you've heard about negative consequences in the past, it's also possible that circumstances have changed. For example, with 46% of 30-to-49-year-olds

sporting tattoos, employers—even if they dislike tattoos personally—may have realized they can't afford to rule out nearly half
their applicants.[3]

What's the Worst That Could Happen?

It's also important to understand the ramifications if you do
decide to show your authentic self at work. For some categories,
the consequences are serious and should be evaluated carefully.
(For instance, the U.S. Supreme Court has ruled that religious
organizations have wide latitude in their employment policies,
and may be able to fire gay employees.[4]) For others, the implications may loom larger in your imagination. Would they fire you
if they knew you enjoyed attending Burning Man? Probably not.
Would it cause them to think you "weren't a cultural fit," slow-
ing down your career progress? Possibly, but you also have the
opportunity to demonstrate in other ways, such as being excel-
lent at your job and building good relationships with colleagues,
that you actually do gel with the corporate culture (provided it's
one that *you'd* like to stay with).

What Would You Do Differently
If You Were Your Real Self?

"I can't be my real self" is a painful yet amorphous feeling.
Pinning down the specifics is useful, however, because certain
elements of self-expression may be easier to attain than you think.
Consider how you would dress, speak, and act differently at work

if you were being your true self. How does that compare with your behavior today? You may still need to wear a suit for work events, for instance, but there's likely room to showcase your creative flair with colorful socks or interesting neckties.

It's also quite possible that your coworkers will respond positively to seeing more of your genuine interests and personality. As I describe in my book *Reinventing You*, former vice president Al Gore was lambasted in the press during the 2000 U.S. presidential race for his campaign's decision to position him as a podium-banging populist crusader rather than his naturally wonky self. He was derided as wooden and inauthentic, and it was only when he returned to his love of environmental policy with the release of the 2006 global warming documentary *An Inconvenient Truth* that he again found his stride.

Is There a Way to Conduct a Pilot?

Finally, if it feels risky to go all in on being yourself at work, think about a small experiment you could try to test the waters. For instance, if you're naturally funny but tamp down your humor at work because "it's not done" at your company, try cracking a few (carefully chosen) jokes one day. See what sort of response you receive. Did others seem to notice? Did you receive any feedback, positive or negative? Turn to a trusted colleague to ask their opinion.

If the response was negative, you've gotten useful information. Fortunately, a small pilot almost certainly won't hurt your long-term career prospects; you can always go back to showcasing your more serious side. But if the response was positive or neutral (i.e., no one really cared), then you can continue your experiment for a week and keep monitoring the reactions. You may, in fact, inspire others and lighten up the entire office with your behavior. It's possible that the somber demeanor wasn't a requirement, but merely a habit that everyone followed in lockstep.

As an independent consultant I have the luxury of telling clients who don't like the "real me" to find another adviser. But over the course of my career, I've also worked in enough jobs and industries to know that, unfortunately, circumstances and economic necessities sometimes dictate that we stay in a job that requires hiding our true selves. That's a damaging situation that should be the exception rather than the rule. If you feel you can't be yourself at work, sometimes that may really be true. But it's important to question our assumptions, because we may discover there's more leeway for self-expression than we had previously imagined.

QUICK RECAP

Sometimes the corporate cultures in which we find ourselves don't match our personalities, which can create painful pressure to conform. How do you know when it's safe to break out of the mold and be your true self at work? Ask yourself four questions:

- What's your evidence for believing you'll be penalized for being yourself?

- What's the worst that could happen—the ramifications if you decide to show your authentic self?

- What exactly would you do differently if you were acting like your real self?

- Is there a way to conduct a pilot before going all-in on being authentic?

Adapted from "What to Do When You Don't Feel Comfortable Being Yourself at Work," on hbr.org, January 29, 2016 (product #H02MNZ).

Why the Model Minority Myth Is So Harmful

by Janice Omadeke

In my early twenties, I was promoted to a senior role in a large, conservative corporation. As a Black woman, I was conscious of needing to fly under the radar and not ruffle any feathers for fear of being seen as "difficult" in a space where my race was considered a key attribute in earning my title.

This was the early 2000s, when messages from the media and society outwardly promoted the concept of poor work-life balance as a badge of honor. It was important to show a codependent and undying dedication to your employer by being the last to leave the office, sacrificing family time, and doing whatever it took to prove that you were serious about your job.

For people of color, this pressure included something that was never said aloud but was a very clear expectation: Make sure any characteristics of a nonwhite American culture that you possess are left at the door when you come to work. Essentially, be a "model minority" so that leaders won't have to adjust their behaviors to create an inclusive environment.

Damaging phrases such as "difficult" or "challenging" were wielded as swords to ensure underrepresented professionals understood that they had a choice—fit into the box we've built for you or find another job.

During this period of my career, I would often seek guidance from non-underrepresented leaders in executive roles, asking how I could best succeed on their teams. I was told to smile more, straighten my hair, buy a designer handbag, and wear high heels. So I did. I dressed in brands deemed professional, did not wear my natural hair to work, and did not address moments of extreme bias or racism that I encountered. My desire to please people, while suppressing my instincts about what was right and wrong as well as my genuine self, led to burnout and dissatisfaction—and I wasn't alone in my experience. (For more on whether to change your appearance for a job, see the sidebar, "Can I Wear My Hair Natural?")

Through my work as the CEO and founder of an HR tech software that increases employee retention through mentorship, I've met countless employees of color who have faced similar biases—in their lives, in their schools, and, yes, in their careers. The Black community is not the only group being affected. My colleague Minh Vu and I recently connected around the damaging, but different, impacts the model minority myth has had on our worlds.

"Growing up as a closeted gay Asian American man in Texas, I felt the need to balance the societal pressure of being a model minority alongside the pressure of living up to what it means to be a man, in order to feel safe in this world," Minh told me. "If that meant I needed to be silent, obedient, and nonthreatening, or be at the top of my class and engaged in math and science, then I tried my best to meet that expectation—and that bled into my behaviors in the office too. I drove myself further in the

Can I Wear My Hair Natural?

by Tina Opie

I was running a workshop on authenticity in the workplace, and a former student, Nadia, asked me, "I see that you wear your hair natural. Do you think it's OK if I wear my hair natural to the workplace?"

I walked her through the decision. "Do you like your natural hair?" I asked. "Yes, I feel good about it. It makes me feel good as a Black, Latina woman. That's what I'd like to do," she replied. Great. We established that her natural hair is connected to her authenticity and identity.

She wanted to go into law, so I said, "Describe for me the kind of context or environment you think you're going to confront in the legal profession." "They're very conservative and wear tailored suits," Nadia replied. She was describing the men, but we quickly realized it was very similar for women.

Here comes the difficult part. There isn't a clear-cut answer. I told Nadia that she has to weigh the consequences: If your hair is authentic to you, and if changing it makes you feel like you're giving up, selling yourself out, or conforming to a point that makes you uncomfortable, then perhaps that's not the best decision. But understand that if you walk into this particular context, it may mean that you don't get the job.   (*continued*)

The alternative is that you conform—cover your hair, straighten it, get rid of any visible evidence of your Africanness or Blackness. You can do that, but if that is going to make you feel bad about yourself, then maybe this company is not the best place for you to be. However, that's a very privileged comment to make, because if you have to pay your bills, you might just have to straighten your hair. You might just have to cover up a tattoo or get rid of your piercings.

I want to get to a place where we are all able to bring who we authentically identify as to the workforce, and where our colleagues and classmates embrace that rather than trying to get us to conform.

––––––

Adapted from "Lead with Authenticity," *Women at Work* podcast, season 1, episode 3, February 9, 2018.

closet and silenced my truth out of fear of wavering from what my coworkers wanted me to be."

Like Minh, I painfully learned that real equity takes work, and that the model minority is a dangerous stereotype that won't help us achieve it.

Understanding the Model Minority Myth

The notion of the model minority has always existed. Coined by William Petersen, a University of California sociologist, the term has often been used to refer to a minority group perceived as particularly successful.[1]

In large, conservative industries, such as finance and management consulting, there's historically been a trend of promoting a small percentage of model minority professionals, who the organization then considers to be sufficient for "equitable representation" on their leadership teams.[2] But even that degree of representation is a stretch at some companies.

Black employees account for just 7% of managers in the U.S. private sector, according to McKinsey's 2021 Race in the Workplace report. Likewise, an analysis of national EEOC workforce data found that Asian American white-collar professionals are the least likely group to be promoted from individual contributor roles into management.[3] All of this data echoes a study by *Forbes* that shows less inclusive leaders have *talent blindness*, "meaning they are less able to recognize employees' unique strengths."[4]

Do you see the problem?

The more all-white leadership teams we have, the more difficult it will be for people at the top to recognize that they have an issue in the first place. Those who hold the most power may not even be aware that they are pressuring their team members to be model minorities.

But they are. The one or two people of color who do make it into senior roles at these organizations often have to overcompensate to ensure that they don't project negative stereotypes. There is huge pressure on their shoulders to assimilate in order to make themselves more palatable to their white team members, along with a fear that, if they don't, their opportunity may be taken away.

Together, these factors lead to increased feelings of isolation at work and also feed into a false myth that there can be only one successful person of color in any organization. For both Minh and myself, it was only when we decided to switch up the game and be free of the model minority trap that we found career happiness.

In my case, this meant learning to own my contributions at work and refusing to accept the calls to make others around me comfortable. In Minh's, it meant sharing his full identity in the office.

"While it's a constant journey to unlearn the ways in which the [model minority myth] has affected my life and work," Minh said, "I remind myself of how it has been used to silence so many of us, including other communities of color. Now I find strength in standing out and proud as a gay first-generation Vietnamese American, and am less fearful in boldly using my voice to stand visible and present in both my work and life."

Based on our experiences, I want to share some advice around how other people of color can move past this harmful myth too.

Finding the Courage to Be Authentically Seen

Before we get into the more practical advice, it's important to understand the workforce as it is today and the challenges you are going to go up against once you enter it.

Legacy companies, particularly in the finance industry, still tend to have outdated thinking and policies in the areas of culture, equity, and inclusion.[5] Inclusivity is about making sure all employees, regardless of background, feel that they are important and valued members of the team. But traditional bias hasn't allowed this to happen, and has led to an intersection of millennials and Gen Zers entering a workforce that is leaving minority professionals behind. In the financial services industry, for example, more than 80% of all employees are white.[6]

This is not only bad for the worker—it's also bad for the business. Professionals of color who feel empowered at work are more likely to bring their authentic voices forward and impact the culture in positive ways. When this happens, companies maintain market advantage. The more diverse perspectives an organization has, the more consumers their products will impact.

All this said, I'm optimistic that things are shifting when it comes to cultural attitudes toward minorities. The pandemic triggered not just a public health crisis but also a technological, social, and cultural disruption, as Microsoft research notes.[7] People are now reflecting more on their self-identities and how they show up in the world. The notion of the model minority has always existed, but Black and Asian American professionals in particular are beginning to challenge the status quo and recognize the negative impact it has on their well-being and career satisfaction.

If you're a young professional of color, how can you avoid the model minority trap and bring your whole courageous self to work early in your career?

Seek out companies with a proven track record

Start early. There are organizations where you don't have to compromise yourself, and you can find opportunities at them. It just might take a little more work at the beginning of your job search.

When applying to jobs, look for companies that are increasing their diversity budgets and have a proven track record of promoting underrepresented professionals, as well as companies that rank highly on diversity and inclusion index reports. Examine their leadership teams to see whether there is equitable representation across multiple identity intersections, which can be a direct indicator of the company's commitment to diversity.

► **PRO TIPS**

- You can find most companies' credentials on their LinkedIn career pages. Are they a celebrated diversity, equity, and inclusion (DEI) employer? Can they support your growth potential? Are there many other people of color in leadership positions?

- Find companies worth applying to by searching for curated lists of organizations that excel in diversity and inclusion or are considered one of the "best places to work" (such as those found on the Great Place to Work website).

Build yourself a support system

Once you've settled into your role, make connections with people who can support you during challenging times and help you navigate your new workplace. This might be a leadership coach, a mentor, or even peers you meet through an employee resource group (ERG). The goal here is to build a support system that can provide you with advice when you face challenges or biases in the office and champion the unique perspectives you have to offer.

Surrounding yourself with allies will give you the courage to show up as your full self, and in turn you'll develop a healthier relationship to your job. This is so important—because who you are at the office is going to impact who you are in your personal life too. If you have shame about how you are presenting yourself at work, it is going to come home with you at the end of the day and negatively influence your mental health. I can speak to this from experience.

> **PRO TIPS**

- If your employer doesn't have in-house mentorship programs or ERGs, look outside of your organization. Resources such as the Plug are great for finding mentors (both within and outside of your company) who can help you navigate the landscape.

- Ask your network if anyone knows of any support groups you can join, or look into connecting with leaders at your company who have exemplified their commitment to diversity and inclusion. You can figure this out by asking around or seeing who shows up to any DEI initiatives.

Have a game plan for addressing bias

While the work of building inclusive environments ultimately falls on leadership teams (not you personally), there are still ways you can prepare yourself for the worst-case scenarios to protect your physical and emotional health. Even after taking the first two steps, you may still confront bias—intentional or not—at your job.

By accepting this from the start, you are removing some of the pain and surprise you may feel if this kind of situation does come up. You are also giving yourself time to prepare.

My advice here is to build a script for how you want to respond to biased comments or assumptions that you encounter during work. Thinking about the tone, language, and message you want to send will empower you to speak out when the moment feels right, and ease the anxiety that often comes with improvising in the moment.

For example, the next time you're asked to share your experiences as an underrepresented founder or team member, respond honestly, highlight that your journey is uniquely yours, and encourage the person asking to continue their research into the larger systemic issues at hand.

Lastly, know that confrontation takes energy, and you may not always be up for it. That's OK. Speak out when it feels energizing to do so—because remaining silent can be draining. Always act within your integrity.

> **PRO TIPS**

- The mentors, peers, and coaches you connect with (along with family and friends) are a good place to go for support. Knowing that these people have your back will make all the difference when, or if, you choose to speak out against a bias that is targeted at either you or someone else.

- Create an identity-confirming space. Fill your work area with pictures, quotes, affirmations, and decorations that remind you of your values. If you're ever challenged with the pressure of filling the role of the model minority, return to this space to affirm your identity. Let it remind you of who you are and encourage you to stay true to yourself.

. . .

Remember, it's only worth staying at a company if you are fulfilled by it. When you are forced to keep quiet and restrain parts of your identity, you're headed down a dark path toward people-pleasing burnout. What's most important at the end of the day is you and your health. A job is just a job, and there will be more of them. It should not be your whole life.

As you take your first steps into the workforce, surround yourself with opportunities that make you feel great, and resist the pressure to conform to old systems and outdated ways of thinking.

QUICK RECAP

People from underrepresented groups often feel they have to act as the "model minority"—to assimilate to make themselves more palatable to their majority-group team members. How can you avoid the model minority trap? Try these tips:

- Apply to jobs at companies that rank highly on diversity and inclusion index reports and have a proven track record of promoting underrepresented professionals.

- Build a support system that can provide you with advice and champion your unique perspectives.

- Prepare yourself for the worst-case scenarios to protect your physical and emotional health.

- Compose a script for how you want to respond to biased comments that you encounter at work.

Adapted from content posted on hbr.org, June 15, 2021.

To learn more about how people of color code-switch at work, read this article:

My Colleagues Can't Get My Name Right

by Talisa Lavarry

What do you do if someone mispronounces your name—or worse, gets it wrong entirely? It's certainly awkward, but it can also be offensive.

HBR received the following note from Horacio (whose name has been disguised to preserve anonymity), asking for advice on this topic. So we asked Talisa Lavarry, author of *Confessions From Your Token Black Colleague* and president of Yum Yum Morale Workplace D.E.I. Strategies, to respond.

Dear HBR,

How does one politely respond when being called by the wrong name? On many occasions, my boss's boss has confused me with another colleague. Although we both have unusual names, our names are very different and do not sound similar at all. There was a particular occasion when my colleague's promotion announcement included a highlight reel of my accomplishments. While I have great respect for my colleague, I still struggle to convey my unique identity.

I suspect race may be a factor in this situation. There's this assumed parochialism that I use to help explain why I feel disconnected from other managers. If I'm honest with myself, I feel disadvantaged in having an unusual name. Is this a projection on my part? Is feeling disadvantaged or marginalized merely a cop-out from initiating and building strong relationships with team members? And is there anything I can do to avoid being confused with my colleague so often?

Sincerely,

Horacio

Dear Horacio,

If anyone can speak about this topic, it is certainly me. I was born in the southern region of the United States—Shreveport, Louisiana, to be exact. My mother named me Talisa. A few years ago, I decided that Tali would be more suitable when it came to seeking employment opportunities and assimilating with my majority white colleagues.

At the time, it felt like the right thing to do. Today I feel differently. While I sincerely like going by Tali, I now realize that making this change just to propel myself in a whitewashed culture wasn't good for me, or any of us bearing names that are perceived as ethnic. Most people don't realize how self-defeating it is to feel like you have to deny parts of yourself in order to be deemed worthy. But pretending to be someone you are not diminishes any chance you have of truly feeling like you belong, and as you have probably discovered, it is taxing.

I appreciate your initiative to propose this question. I believe it is proof that we are growing and changing for the better. More and more of us are realizing the damage that comes with losing such an essential part of ourselves as a way to fit into cultures that were not designed for us to begin with.

Creating this kind of dialogue is necessary if we are to pursue a more just and equitable world. Here is my advice.

Recognize This for What It Is

My answer to your first questions is no, you are not projecting or looking for a cop-out. Sadly, you are dealing with a situation that is common for many people of color. Any history book (or news channel) will show you that white people are often comfortable overlooking and minimizing the value of people of color. There is an unspoken belief that people of color should be happy to be invited to sit at the table. This is true, too, in the work environment: Our white colleagues rarely go out of their way to make sure we are comfortable once seated.

Despite it being illegal, people of color face all kinds of discrimination at work, but not every gesture is obvious. A microaggression, which is what it sounds like you are facing, is much more subtle. Failing to properly identify Black, brown, and other marginalized employees—again and again without concern—is a prime example of one.

Getting a name wrong may be unintentional. In fact, most of the time, it's probably not done with ill intent. That doesn't make it any less irresponsible and unprofessional. It shows blatant disregard for a person's identity, and it sends a message that the culprit deems themselves superior to that person.

Your dilemma seems to be twofold. Mispronouncing your name is one thing. But continuously getting you mixed up with another colleague in the office is downright brazen. I must say that the notion that people from certain groups all look alike is extremely annoying. Still, it continues to happen—a lot. In 2019 the *Washington Post* published a tweet asking people of color about their experiences with being misidentified in predominantly white environments.[1] More than 400 people replied with their stories.

It's important that you are aware of this reality. Stepping outside of your experience, viewing it in this larger context, and recognizing it as another result of systemic racism will make a world of difference in how you both feel about and approach the situation.

Know That It's Not About You

We've already established that getting someone's name wrong can feel like a sign of disrespect, but there's a big chance that it is coming from a place of unconscious bias. You need to know this to protect your mental health. Harboring anger against your colleagues will not benefit you at all; neither will it aid the growth of the people doing you harm.

Do your best to separate yourself from their behaviors. I know that this is easier said than done, but if you fail to create the distance you need to gain clarity, you put yourself in a dangerous position. The last thing you want to do is change yourself instead of confronting the actual problem.

There is no amount of covering or code-switching that will impress the people doing you harm. As daunting as it may sound, you must continue to remind yourself that this situation is not about you. There is nothing wrong with who you are, and you have nothing to be ashamed of.

You mentioned that you "struggle to display your unique identity" at work, which causes me to believe that you are in an environment that doesn't feel so inclusive to you. I also know that being your authentic self at work—especially as a person of color in corporate America—comes with risks. At the same time, I do believe you will feel better and work better once you determine and feel confident projecting your personal style.

The first step to showing more of yourself is being honest with your colleagues about how their mistakes make you feel.

Call Out Your Colleagues (Gently)

While correcting someone in a position of power may make you feel like you are being overly assertive, you are not. Our names are a huge part of our identities. We should all be willing to get the names of our colleagues right. There are a few ways you can (gently) call someone out.

Ask clarifying questions

You can do this without sounding condescending. The next time someone addresses you by the wrong name, offer a warm smile while saying something like, "Wait, did you just call me [name] by accident?" This lets the person know that you care about having your name said correctly, and it gives them the opportunity to (hopefully) apologize and confirm the correct name or pronunciation.

Offer a correction

If you're not comfortable calling someone out in the moment, practice in the mirror first, or role-play with a friend, a career coach, or a therapist.

For instance, you might rehearse explaining your name in a memorable way: "My name is Horacio. The H is silent, and being that I'm the finance lead, it probably won't be hard to remember that I deal with ratios." Or sound it out for the other person: "My name is Talisa, by the way. Just think Lisa with a Ta in front of it."

If you are called the name of your colleague again, try: "[Name] actually works in marketing and sits over by the kitchen. I'm not sure why you are getting us mixed up, but I want to be sure that you know that I am the one who sits here, by the window."

Do it in writing

Include the phonetic spelling of your name when presenting it in writing. This can be done on written memos or in email signatures.

Garner support from allies

These conversations can be emotionally draining, and the more support you have, the better. Your allies are the people who can speak up for you and correct others when you are not around, or do so in moments when you are present but may not be comfortable or have the energy to say something yourself.

Find peers or colleagues whom you trust, and casually explain the situation to them. Garnering the support of someone who has more stature than you will be especially helpful. Your well-tenured colleagues may have the power to advocate for you when speaking to leaders throughout the company, which could result in an even more impactful cultural change.

Lastly, notice what's going on. You might be surprised by how many of your peers are experiencing similar microaggressions. I've personally found these kinds of situations easier to navigate when I'm doing it with people who can identify with what I'm going through.

Directly Express Your Concerns

If the above approaches don't yield any results, it is time to be blunt in your delivery. You don't have to physically express emotions like anger or sadness to show that you are upset, but you do have to clearly communicate how your colleagues' mistakes make you feel.

Simply say, "My name is Horacio, and I'd really appreciate you saying it correctly." After you have said this, stop and allow them to respond. Hopefully, this will open the door to a longer conversation and give the other person an opportunity to apologize and verbally commit to saying your name correctly moving forward.

Make a Formal Complaint

Let's say you have tried to have a direct conversation, and even after that the issue continues. Now it's time to submit your concerns to human resources. You may be able to do so anonymously, but this is totally contingent on your work environment and the overall relationship between you and the person or persons who have refused to pronounce your name properly.

No matter how you decide to go about filing the complaint, be sure to let HR know the steps that you have already taken to resolve the issue. Give examples of the consequences that this kind of microaggression can create: stress, anxiety, feelings of isolation, and depression—all of which can impact your work performance.

Tell HR exactly how they can make sure it doesn't happen again. If you feel comfortable doing so, you might even propose the organization invest in some form of race and diversity training for all employees, or suggest that leadership mention the importance of properly identifying colleagues in the next companywide meeting.

Know When to Leave

You are responsible for the personal care of yourself, your health, your career growth, and your sanity. While walking away from a position you enjoy may be painful, if you constantly have to perform to feel seen, heard, valued, and respected, you may ultimately want to consider moving on.

There are a great deal of offenses taking place within workplaces across the world, but there are more and more companies that are embracing the concept of creating and nurturing diverse, equitable, and inclusive environments. We are all deserving of opportunities to be ourselves while offering up our best work.

QUICK RECAP

Getting a name wrong may be unintentional, but that doesn't make it any less irresponsible and unprofessional. So what should you do if your colleagues keep messing up your name?

- Know that this is about them, not you.

- Ask clarifying questions or offer a correction: "Wait, did you just call me [name] by accident?"

- If the previous attempt doesn't work, be blunt: "My name is [your name], and I'd really appreciate you saying it correctly."

- Find allies to support you, as these conversations can be emotionally draining.

- If the issue continues after a direct conversation, submit your concerns to human resources.

Adapted from "Ask an Expert: My Colleagues Can't Get My Name Right," on hbr.org, February 10, 2021.

How to Have Difficult Conversations Without Burning Bridges

by Evelyn Nam

Imagine these scenarios:

- A senior executive in your organization makes a sexist comment in a companywide email.

- The CEO has made it clear that your company will not be investing in sustainability, an issue that you care deeply about.

- You witness a microaggression in a team meeting.

In each of these instances, your instinct may be to speak up, confront the person, and share your views. But what's the effective way to do so?

When you're just entering the workforce, it can feel challenging to contribute to an organization's company policies or vocalize your thoughts on issues that matter to you. Your lack of positional power may discourage you from being honest or giving feedback. The problem with this mindset is that it ignores how important our values are to our well-being at work. In fact, according to a global survey of 2,600 Gen Zers, only one in five would work for a company that doesn't share their values. Similarly, at least 70% of Gen Zers involve themselves in a social or political cause.[1] Further, there is evidence that people who are able to link their social purpose to their jobs are more satisfied and engaged at work.[2]

To better understand how you can let your voice be heard and have difficult conversations at work without burning bridges, I spoke with some experts. Here's what they had to say.

See Others as Potential Allies, Not Adversaries

When sharing your thoughts about an incident, such as a micro-aggression, approach the person who made the comment as an ally. Social advocacy is more effective when you start with "calling people in" to dialogue instead of "calling them out" or simply critiquing them.

Todd Kashdan, author of *The Art of Insubordination*, says that calling in is ultimately about admitting that we're all of the same nature. "We all have flaws, make mistakes, and often don't have the energy or mental capacity to do the things we care about. What's important is we acknowledge it and choose to do better," Kashdan explains.

Your goal should be to have a conversation and try to understand the other person's perspective. During the discussion, the emphasis needs to be on helping them understand their mistake rather than trying to shame them for it. For instance, you could say, "I didn't understand the joke you made. Honestly, it was a bit hurtful to hear as a person of [the identity you hold]. Would you be open to a conversation about this?"

Trying to have this conversation, Kashdan says, is not just ideologically wise—it's pragmatic and practical. When you invite another person to discuss an issue rather than trying to win a battle, they're more likely to listen and move forward from the conversation positively.

"Things are a lot less likely to get done in an adversarial setup. That's why it's strategic to set up an equal ground where both people can talk," says Tobias Berkman, a senior associate at the Consensus Building Institute and an affiliated faculty member of the Program on Negotiation at Harvard Law School.

Listen to the Other Person's Views

Once you're on equal footing, it's important to listen to and consider the other person's point of view. Research shows that we often exaggerate how extreme our opponents are.[3]

"Somebody says something, and all of a sudden we create this whole construct about who they are as a person and what type of intention they have, and then we proceed as if that's true," says Julia Minson, an associate professor at Harvard Kennedy School. "That automatically sets up the adversarial environment in which someone has to lose." She explains that it's important to learn more about the other person's actual intent, rather than filling it in with your own assumptions.

To clarify those intentions, listen actively and be curious. "Listening doesn't mean compromising. It means truly understanding where the other person is coming from," Minson says. "Spend time trying to understand why the other person believes what they believe."

You can also ask specific questions to better understand intent. For example, open the conversation with, "Tell me more about your perspective on what happened." Pay attention to what the other person says. After listening thoroughly, paraphrase what you heard: "I understand what you said is XYZ. Did I get that right?" This will help you clarify misconceptions and confirm the facts. Based on this information, you can follow up with your point of view: "Listening to you speak made me think of this new piece of research on the gap in health insurance for nonpartnered folks that I wanted to share with you."

Asking questions can also help you learn more about where the actual gaps are between your beliefs. Is their view based on personal experience, or perhaps the lack of it? Are they aware of information that contradicts your research? Do they seem open to new information and show an affinity to change? Paying attention to these things can help you come up with solutions that are acceptable to everyone.

Minson says that when we listen and others feel heard, they're much more likely to hear us: "The norm of reciprocity—I do unto you what you do unto me—is a basic human behavior. That will enable the other person to open up the floor to you, making it easier for us to convey our stance."

Alison Wood Brooks, an associate professor at Harvard Business School, adds that intent isn't just about the other person's actions. It's also about your own intentions. Ask yourself: What is my goal in reaching out to this person to have a conversation?

If your aim is to create some type of change in the person and to get your point across, then you need to remember that even in the heat of the moment, Brooks explains.

If you simply want to confront someone, share your anger, and make a point, however, it might only escalate the situation.

Remember That You're Dealing with Another Human

Throughout this conversation, it's important to remember that you're communicating with a person who has feelings, stories, a history, trauma, a heart, and the same needs as you: to be heard, understood, and, most importantly, respected. Kashdan says that the now-common, overused practice of labeling people as narcissistic, gaslighting, and toxic can make us dehumanize others, especially when their opinions don't reflect our values.

That's why it's important to listen to others and understand their point of view. Humans have the ability to change and improve themselves. Minson highlights that when we see that potential in those we disagree with, we're likely to engage with them more effectively. It's important to avoid seeing people as "good" or "bad." This will help you extend some grace and empathy to the other person.

On the other hand, exclusion can lead to more extreme views. If the other person feels alienated, they may end up seeking out and finding others who will listen to them and agree with their point of view. This further isolates us from each other and creates polarizing opinions and thoughts, Minson adds. Viewing the other person as human (albeit one with flaws) with the same fundamental need to be heard and respected can go a long way in creating the change we want to see.

It's OK to Use Humor (Sometimes)

It may seem counterintuitive, but Kashdan says that a sense of humor can help tremendously in social advocacy. He shares the example of Loretta Ross, a professor and an activist, who wrote in an op-ed piece in the *New York Times*: "In 2017, as a college professor in Massachusetts, I accidentally misgendered a student of mine during a lecture. I froze in shame, expecting to be blasted. Instead, my student said, 'That's all right; I misgender myself sometimes.' We need more of this kind of grace."[4]

Kashdan contrasts this with using shame or embarrassment as a persuasion tactic. "When you shame others, you drive them into a corner, and all they can do in that situation is to either coil up or scratch your eyeballs. You want to give them an out," he says. Humor allows us to be human, disarm others, and save face. It calls people in and doesn't assume negative intent.

That said, humor is something you can practice only if you feel comfortable and safe with the people you're interacting with. It also depends on the situation and the values that are being challenged. Humor can be most useful while speaking up to a colleague that you get along with who has committed a micro-aggression. In situations where you're speaking to power, humor can be challenging. Assess who you can use humor as a tool with, and ensure that it helps you move the conversation forward instead of insulting or degrading the other person.

Don't Be Afraid to Ask for Help

All of this advice may be helpful if you're addressing a single issue with a colleague or even your boss. But what if you're eager to share your perspective about a larger organizational issue? Or what if the person you need to confront is the CEO or another senior leader?

This might seem like an impossible task, but don't get discouraged. Amit Goldenberg, an associate professor at Harvard Business School, explains that in such instances, finding allies is an important strategy in getting your voice heard.

To find allies, think about the people in leadership positions who care about the same issues. Can you ask your boss for advice on how to move forward? Can you connect with a leader in your department who is closer to the CEO? Are there senior managers in other departments who you'd feel comfortable seeking feedback from on how to move forward?

Once you have two to three people you're ready to approach, set up a meeting and explain how you feel about the given situation. Think of yourself as an advocate for the cause, and pitch how taking certain steps would help the company, its leaders, and its employees.

For example, you could say something like, "I read the CEO's recent address on our strategy for the year, and I felt like we missed the opportunity to focus on ESG. With sustainability gaining popularity across different industries, I believe it's an opportune moment for our organization to pursue clients who prioritize ESG goals because of XYZ. Here are my ideas on what we can do better. I'd love to either write an email to the CEO about this or have a senior leader bring it up in the executive meeting. How do you suggest I move forward?"

. . .

Advocating for a more humane world that's built on care and respect is not easy, and you ultimately have little control over how others respond to you. But even if your attempts to engage another person are not always successful, remind yourself that you made a wholehearted effort, and that's what counts. In the end, the key to changing minds and behaviors is patience—you must give it time.

QUICK RECAP

When you have a situation that requires speaking up or confronting your colleagues, what's the best way to voice your concerns?

- See others as potential allies, not adversaries. "Call people in" instead of "calling them out."

- Be curious about the other person's point of view. Ask specific questions to better understand their intent.

- Extend some grace and empathy to the other person.

- Use humor to disarm others and save face—but only if you feel comfortable and safe with the person you're interacting with.

- Find allies and be an advocate. Pitch to leadership how taking certain steps would help the company and its employees.

Adapted from content posted on hbr.org, May 19, 2023.

To learn how to control your emotions during a difficult conversation, watch this video:

Are You Living a Double Life on Social Media?

by Paige Cohen

Bisi Alimi is done living a double life.

It's been a journey, literally, across land and sea.

Today he is an executive coach and the founder of the Bisi Alimi Foundation, which advocates for the rights of LGBTQ+ people in the Nigerian workforce. In 2004 he was an actor and activist in Lagos, and the first man in his country to come out as gay on national TV.

When I first came across Alimi on LinkedIn, I knew nothing about his story. That day I logged into my account with the regular expectations: the bright landing page, the long list of updates, and my connections, clad in crisp attire, grinning as I scrolled through the feed. I didn't expect Alimi, fierce and unapologetic, serving realness over a baby-pink background in a leather tube top, a black tutu, and thigh-high boots.

"Do we live a double social media life?" his post began. "As someone who has a lot to do with the corporate world, I have really struggled [with] representation . . . How do I show myself on LinkedIn in a way that doesn't cost me jobs? Why do I have to be a different person on different social media platform[s]?"[1]

In my own profile picture, I stand smiling in a button-up and suspenders. A green field sprawls blurrily in the background. The photo was taken at a wedding I attended, and I chose it because it is one of the rare moments I've been captured in anything close to a traditional business suit.

In real life, I'm covered in gray-and-black tattoos. My hair oscillates along a spectrum of colors, and if I don't mat it down with gel, I look like an electrified cartoon. I prefer ripped jeans over chinos, patterned vests to shirts, and love anything with glitter, including combat boots. Few of these preferences feel truly "safe for work" or any online platform where a recruiter might find me.

Alimi had hit a personal note, for me and others. More than 60 people commented on his post, many expressing similar pressures to present a different, more subdued version of themselves in work-related settings. What struck me most was that the responses touched on points far beyond physical appearance. For a lot of people, it's not just about how we dress; it's about who we fundamentally are. Here are just a few of the comments Alimi received:

> "My professional self has always been separated from my personal, to the detriment, at times, of my success and mental health."

> "I'm nonbinary and autistic and am very honest about myself on other platforms, and have really tried on here too. I've tried to push against this pressure to be conventionally

'professional' on LinkedIn a lot and I've posted . . . my poetry, my gender-bending modelling . . . but people often ignore it."

"I think I literally said the other day, 'I don't know how to exist in different spaces as the same myself.' It's a feeling of never being whole."

"On my WhatsApp I'm quite a different person. I'm more outspoken, more raw, but here I'm very professional."

I wanted to learn more about what inspired Alimi to post that morning. His answer is nuanced and born out of a longer story that he shared with me over the phone while driving through London, where he now resides with his partner and family. It is a story that began several years prior, in Nigeria.

Alimi was born in Lagos, his father a police officer and his mother a cleaner. He went to university to study theater arts, and shortly after graduating he got his first big gig acting on national television. By that point he was already well practiced at living two lives.

"I couldn't talk about my sexuality," he told me. "I come from a culture where being gay is a crime, and it would cost me my job. I had to be intentional about hiding that part of myself. I would go on set and perform both on- and off-camera. I'd flirt with a girl in the workplace, and on the weekends I would go to gay clubs."

Over the years Alimi had lost several of his close friends to HIV, and in 2004 he tested positive for the virus. By then he had gotten involved in activism and mobilization work in Nigeria, promoting safe sex in his community, but he was still publicly closeted and very frightened. "I had already lost so many people," he said. "But it was [the death of] my best friend who really touched me. I began to ask questions around life and death and aspiration and purpose. People were trying to out me, so I took it upon myself. I came out on one of the most-watched talk shows in the country."

Three years later, in 2007, he was forced to flee Nigeria after receiving death threats in response to his disclosure, and so began his work in the United Kingdom. He was granted asylum in 2008, and he earned a master's degree in global governance and public policy from Birkbeck College, University of London, in 2011—marking the beginning of his current path and his work creating more inclusive work environments for LGBTQ+ people in Nigeria.

"Nigeria is a very patriarchal society," Alimi said. "To do the work that I do now, to have this conversation around inclusion with executives and corporations, I have to come across as manly to be respected. A lot of my clients are on LinkedIn, which means to be seen as responsible in my appearances, I have to look formal. But on Instagram, where I have a very young following, I feel comfortable sharing a much freer part of myself, one that challenges the binary."

What if one of his clients stumbled onto Instagram and saw him in heels and a crop top? Would it cost him his job in the same way coming out had years before? Alimi told me he thinks it would bring his professionalism into question.

For Alimi, the question has now become: Is he acting on what he is preaching?

"I'm asking companies if they allow people to come to the office just the way that they are," he said. "Meanwhile, I'm hiding. So, the morning I shared the post of me in a crop top, I had an epiphany. I asked myself: How many other people feel like this? I posted the picture on LinkedIn. The response has only been positive."

The internal dilemma Alimi faced that morning highlights just how outdated certain business practices can be. Even in environments that preach equity and have laws protecting employees from discrimination, many corporations adhere to an old set of rules that favor gendered dress codes with roots in the 18th century. Corporations that hold steadfast to these rules may—knowingly or not—be a major source of stress for gender-nonconforming people or anyone who challenges the gender binary.

I asked Alimi if he has any advice for others facing the double-life dilemma—especially when it comes to how we present ourselves on social media. Should we be hiding who we are for the sake of our employers, or do we need to push the boundaries if we want to change the rules?

"You have to be very careful," Alimi said. "Especially to young people who may be navigating this for the first time, I would tell them to test the waters. Just because a company has an inclusive policy doesn't mean that people in power don't question it and won't have opinions about you. LinkedIn is for professionals. It's where you display your career. It's where you show what you hope to become and who you aspire to be. For me, that's very important. So, ask yourself, How do you think of your career? How do you link your authentic self to the message you are trying to send?"

Alimi's LinkedIn post was tied to the change he is trying to make. It feeds directly into the direction he wishes to take his work and career. Now a graduate of business and executive coaching from Meyler Campbell, he is on a mission to use the power of coaching to cultivate collective intelligence and empathic leadership with a focus on emerging economies. He believes DEI should leave no one behind, and to do this, it needs to develop a global language that transcends religion, culture, and social expectations. He believes we need to take a closer look at the values guiding the powers that be in the corporate world and reimagine those that may be harming marginalized communities.

He was careful to reiterate, though, that some people do not yet have the platform or privilege to show their full selves on social media without consequence. As made clear by the comments on his post, when it comes to representation at work, fashion is just the tip of the iceberg. While identity in and of itself goes much deeper than how we dress, how we present is a factor that we can, to some extent, control. On platforms like LinkedIn, our pictures are our first impressions.

For some of us, the reality is that we still need to be careful about the parts of ourselves we share publicly—for our safety and for our careers. This may not be our reality forever, but it does mean we need to be strategic as we push for the changes we want to see.

"I think LinkedIn is starting something revolutionary in a way," Alimi said. "There's beginning to be a lot of pushback when it comes to what is acceptable in terms of corporate identity, and LinkedIn is where that conversation is starting. We need to take it into the workplace next. The idea of masculinity and femininity is changing. Why are we still operating in a binary structure? It's a question that needs to be at the forefront."

QUICK RECAP

Do you find yourself sharing different parts of yourself on different social media platforms? It's time to redefine what it means to look "professional" online. Remember these points:

- Even in environments that preach equity and have laws protecting employees from discrimination, many corporations adhere to an old set of rules that favor gendered dress codes.

- Corporations that hold steadfast to these rules may—knowingly or not—be a major source of stress for gender-nonconforming people or anyone who challenges the gender binary.

- Ideas of masculinity and femininity are changing, so why are we still operating in a binary structure? This question needs to be at the forefront of the conversation.

Adapted from content posted on hbr.org, October 8, 2021.

NOTES

Chapter 3

1. Lynne C. Giles et al., "Effect of Social Networks on 10 Year Survival in Very Old Australians: The Australian Longitudinal Study of Aging," *Journal of Epidemiology & Community Health* 59, no. 7 (2005): 574–579; Raymond T. Sparrowe et al., "Social Networks and the Performance of Individuals and Groups," *Academy of Management Journal* 44, no. 2 (2001): 316–325; James S. House, Karl R. Landis, and Debra Umberson, "Social Relationships and Health," *Science* 241, no. 4865 (1988): 540–545.

Chapter 6

1. Kausalya Ganesh and Amanda Lazar, "The Work of Workplace Disclosure: Invisible Chronic Conditions and Opportunities for Design," *Proceedings of the ACM on Human-Computer Interaction* 5 (2021).

Chapter 7

1. Michael Cherny, "Hi, I'm Mike. And today is my first day living my truth," LinkedIn, 2019, https://www.linkedin.com/posts/mcherny_hi-im-mike -and-today-is-my-first-day-activity-6488402596557045760-_jEv.

2. Dan Avery, "LGBTQ Rights Fight Reignited 4 Years after N.C.'s 'Bathroom Bill' Controversy," NBC News, December 8, 2020, https://www.nbcnews.com /feature/nbc-out/lgbtq-rights-fight-reignited-4-years-after-n-c-s-n1250390.

Chapter 8

1. Morgan A. Krannitz et al., "Workplace Surface Acting and Marital Partner Discontent: Anxiety and Exhaustion Spillover Mechanisms," *Journal of Occupational Health Psychology* 20, no. 3 (2015): 314–325.

Chapter 11

1. Robert Half, "Cry Me a River: How Emotions Are Perceived in the Workplace," press release, April 3, 2018, https://press.roberthalf.com/2018-04 -03-Cry-Me-A-River-How-Emotions-Are-Perceived-In-The-Workplace.

2. Bianca P. Acevedo et al., "The Highly Sensitive Brain: An fMRI Study of Sensory Processing Sensitivity and Response to Others' Emotions," *Brain and Behavior* 4, no. 4 (2014): 580–594.

3. Half, "Cry Me a River."

4. Brett S. Torrence and Shane Connelly, "Emotion Regulation Tendencies and Leadership Performance: An Examination of Cognitive and Behavioral Regulation Strategies," *Frontiers in Psychology* 10 (2019).

5. Daniel Goleman, "What Makes a Leader?," *Harvard Business Review*, January 2004, https://hbr.org/2004/01/what-makes-a-leader.

6. Elizabeth Baily Wolf et al., "Managing Perceptions of Distress at Work: Reframing Emotion as Passion," *Organizational Behavior and Human Decision Processes* 137 (2016): 1–12.

Chapter 12

1. Sylvia Ann Hewlett and Karen Sumberg, "For LGBT Workers, Being 'Out' Brings Advantages," *Harvard Business Review*, July–August 2011, https://hbr.org/2011/07/for-lgbt-workers-being-out-brings-advantages.

2. Dorie Clark and Christie Smith, "Help Your Employees Be Themselves at Work," hbr.org, November 3, 2014, https://hbr.org/2014/11/help-your-employees -be-themselves-at-work.

3. Katherine Schaeffer and Shradha Dinesh, "32% of Americans Have a Tattoo, Including 22% Who Have More Than One," Pew Research Center, August 15, 2023, https://www.pewresearch.org/short-reads/2023/08/15/32-of -americans-have-a-tattoo-including-22-who-have-more-than-one/.

4. Richard Wolf, "Supreme Court Upholds Autonomy of Religious Employers in Employment Discrimination Cases," *USA Today*, July 8, 2020, https://www.usatoday.com/story/news/politics/2020/07/08/supreme-court-says -religious-school-teachers-cannot-sue-over-firings/3207815001/.

Chapter 13

1. Sapna Cheryan and Galen V. Bodenhausen, "Model Minority," in Stephen M. Caliendo and Charlton D. McIlwain, eds., *Routledge Companion to Race and Ethnicity* (New York: Routledge, 2011), 173–176.

2. Pippa Stevens, "Companies Are Making Bold Promises About Greater Diversity, But There's a Long Way to Go," CNBC, June 11, 2020, https://www .cnbc.com/2020/06/11/companies-are-making-bold-promises-about-greater -diversity-theres-a-long-way-to-go.html.

3. Buck Gee and Denise Peck, "Asian Americans Are the Least Likely Group in the U.S. to Be Promoted to Management," hbr.org, May 31, 2018, https://hbr.org/2018/05/asian-americans-are-the-least-likely-group-in-the-u-s-to -be-promoted-to-management.

4. Kim Brimhall, "Employees Sound Off on What Makes a Truly Inclusive Leader," *Fast Company*, September 27, 2020, https://www.fastcompany.com/90555716/employees-sound-off-on-what-makes-a-truly-inclusive-leader.

5. Laura Noonan and Taylor Nicole Rogers, "Share of Black Employees in Senior US Finance Roles Falls Despite Diversity Efforts," *Financial Times*, March 31, 2021, https://www.ft.com/content/887d064a-bd5e-4ce6-9671-9057e12bd5c7.

6. Alessandra Malito, "Three Reasons You Don't See Many People of Color in the Financial Services Industry—and How to Fix It," MarketWatch, July 8, 2020, https://www.marketwatch.com/story/three-reasons-you-dont-see-many-people-of-color-in-the-financial-services-industry-and-how-to-fix-it-2020-06-11.

7. Microsoft, "The New Future of Work," https://www.microsoft.com/en-us/research/project/the-new-future-of-work.

Chapter 14

1. Rachel Hatzipanagos, "It 'Makes You Feel Invisible,'" *Washington Post*, May 2, 2019, https://www.washingtonpost.com/nation/2019/05/02/co-workers-keep-mixing-up-people-color-office-its-more-than-mistake.

Chapter 15

1. HeForShe and Lewis, "New Rules: How Is Gen Z Changing the World of Work," May 2021, https://www.heforshe.org/sites/default/files/2021-05/lewis-genz-report-final.pdf; Jackie Cooper, "Unleashing the Power of Gen Z," Edelman, December 20, 2021, https://www.edelman.com/insights/unleashing-power-gen-z.

2. Bea Boccalandro, "Increasing Employee Engagement Through Corporate Volunteering," Voluntare, 2019, https://www.beaboccalandro.com/wp-content/uploads/2019/01/Engagement-Report-Voluntare_eng_04122018-2.pdf.

3. Brian P. Reschke et al., "Mutual Receptiveness to Opposing Views Bridges Ideological Divides in Network Formation," October 2020, http://dx.doi.org/10.2139/ssrn.3703958.

4. Loretta Ross, "I'm a Black Feminist. I Think Call-Out Culture Is Toxic," *New York Times*, August 17, 2019, https://www.nytimes.com/2019/08/17/opinion/sunday/cancel-culture-call-out.html.

Chapter 16

1. Bisi Alimi, "Do we live a double social media life? As someone who has a lot to do with the corporate world, I have really struggled about representation and the idea of . . . ," LinkedIn, https://www.linkedin.com/posts/bisialimi_do-we-live-a-double-social-media-life-activity-6817857337181708288-ITNd.

INDEX

advocating for policy changes, 61–62
Alimi, Bisi, 143–149
allies
  in difficult conversations, 134–135,
    139–140
  in model minority myth, 118–119
  in name misidentification,
    128–129
  in self-doubt, 86–87
apologizing for crying, 98
asking
  for help, 139–140
  for pronouns, 36
  questions, 127–128, 136
authenticity
  challenges in, xiv
  in conversation, 25–29
  creativity and, xv
  defined, xiii
  discomfort with, 105–110
  on social media, 143–149

being yourself. See authenticity;
  identity
Berkman, Tobias, 135
bias
  neurodivergence and, 52
  racial, 113–114
  responses to, 119–121
  unconscious, 126–127
boundaries
  to avoid oversharing, 9–12
  when coming out as transgender,
    68–69
  when forming relationships, 28–29

breath control, 99
Brooks, Alison Wood, 136–137
Browne, Harrison, 59, 67–68
bullying, 52, 65–66, 100
Butler, Madison, xi–xv

calming yourself, 99
changing pronouns, 33–34. See also
  pronouns
Chaplin, Lan Nguyen, 3–14
Cherny, Michael, 57–71
cisgender people, sharing pronouns
  and, 37
Clark, Dorie, 105–110
Clark, Rachel, 59, 60, 63, 67
Cohen, Paige, 31–38, 143–149
cohesion, in groups, 39–40
coming out as transgender, 57–71
  advocating for policy changes,
    61–62
  boundaries, setting, 68–69
  calculating risks of, 59–60
  dealing with others' reactions,
    64–66
  mental health management, 63–64
  personal conversations, 62–63
  physical/emotional changes, 66
  recognizing the void, 69–70
  researching information on,
    60–61
  spotlight management, 67–68
communication. See conversations;
  difficult conversations
company events, 41–42
complaints, filing formal, 130

consequences, of authenticity at work, 107
context, of vulnerability, 8–9
conversations
    authenticity in, 25–29
    coming out as transgender, 62–63
    deep listening in, 12–13
    difficult, 133–141
    See also difficult conversations
correcting
    name misidentification, 127–129
    pronouns, 35–36, 65
Cozma, Irina, 15–21
Creative Act, The (Ruben), xv
creativity, authenticity and, xv
criticism, taking personally, 90
crying at work, 95–101
    apologizing for, 98
    following up after, 98–99

David, Sophia, 59, 61–62
David, Susan, 75–79
deadnaming, 67, 69
deep acting, 76–77
deep listening, 12–13
defining values, 18–19, 21
dehumanizing others, avoiding, 137–138
DEI (diversity, equity, inclusion) employers, 117–118
difficult conversations, 133–141
    allies in, 134–135, 139–140
    humanizing others, 137–138
    humor in, 138
    listening, 135–137
    values and well-being, 134
disclosing
    invisible marginalized identities, 47–56
    neurodivergence, 52–53
    self-disclosure, 39–45

See also coming out as transgender; sharing pronouns
discomfort, with authenticity at work, 105–110
discrimination
    legal recourse for, 50–51
    model minority myth, 111–122
    name misidentification, 123–131
    researching information on, 60–61
discursive framing, 34–35
Dudtschak, Katherine (Katie), 59, 63–65, 69
DuVally, Maeve, 59, 61–65, 68–69

emotional intelligence, 97
emotional investment in job, 90–91
emotional labor, 75–79
emotional/physical changes (for transgender people), managing, 66
experiments, conducting small, 108–109

failing, fear of, 84–85
fairness, as value, 19
family, as value, 19–20
fear of failing, 84–85
filing complaints, to HR, 130
finding values, 16–17, 21
follow-up, after crying at work, 98–99
Fountain, Dannie Lynn, 47–56
freedom, as value, 18

gender identity
    coming out as transgender, 57–71
    sharing pronouns, 31–38
    on social media, 143–149

Goldenberg, Amit, 139
Gore, Al, 108
gravitas, 6
Gupta, Shalene, 57–71

"have to" thinking, 78
Heighes, Owen, 59, 62, 65, 68
help, asking for, 139–140
helpfulness, 27–28, 91
Hewlett, Sylvia Ann, 106
hiding true self, 105–110, 145, 147
honesty, 16–17, 20
HR (human resources), formal
    complaints to, 130
humanizing others, 137–138
humor, 35, 138

identifying strengths, 5–6
identity
    consequences of hiding, 106
    invisible marginalized, 47–56
    job roles versus, 89–94
    See also gender identity; racial
        identity
identity-confirming spaces, 121
imposter syndrome, 81–88
inclusivity, 116
Inconvenient Truth, An (documen-
    tary), 108
intent, 135–137
interviews, 50–51
invisible marginalized identities,
    47–56
    how to disclose, 51, 54–55
    in interviews, 50–51
    when to disclose, 49–51
Ivowi, Tucci, 81–88

job crafting, 78
job roles, identity versus, 89–94

Kashdan, Todd, 134–135, 137–138
Kersey, Amanda, 39–45

Lavarry, Talisa, 123–131
legal recourse for discrimination,
    50–51
LinkedIn, 143–149
listening
    deep listening, 12–13
    in difficult conversations, 135–137
    in forming relationships, 27–28

Maisonneuve, Ry, 59, 63
McPherson, Susan, 25–29
mental health, managing during
    coming out, 63–64
microaggressions, 49, 67, 125, 130, 138
Minson, Julia, 135–136, 137
misidentification by name. See name
    misidentification
model minority myth, 111–122
    responses to bias due to, 119–121
    support system, building, 118–119
multiple pronouns, 37

Nam, Evelyn, 133–141
name misidentification, 123–131
    correcting, 127–129
    HR (human resources) complaints,
        130
    systemic racism and, 125–126
    unconscious bias in, 126–127
natural hair, 113–114
nervousness, acknowledging, 83–84
neurodivergence, disclosing, 52–53
nonbinary, 32, 65–66

O'Brien, Tim, 89–94
Omadeke, Janice, 111–122

Opie, Tina, 113–114
optimism, as value, 19
oversharing, avoiding, 9–12

peer coaches, 86–87
penalties, for being yourself, 106–107
people-pleasers, 91
personal philosophy, 10–11
Petersen, William, 114
Phillips, Katherine W., 39–45
phonetic spellings, of names, 128
physical/emotional changes (for trans-
    gender people), managing, 66
pilot tests, 108–109
policy changes, advocating for, 61–62
professional development, 84–85
pronouns
    asking for, 36
    cisgender people and, 37
    changing, 33–34
    correcting, 35–36, 65
    in email and online, 33
    multiple, 37
    sharing, 31–38

questions, asking, 127–128, 136

racial identity
    model minority myth, 111–122
    name misidentification, 123–131
    natural hair, 113–114
    self-disclosure and, 41–45
ranking values, 17
recency effect, 98
reciprocity, 136
recognizing the void, when coming
    out as transgender, 69–70
reflecting on values, 16–17
Reinventing You (Clark), 108
relationships

forming, 6, 25–29
    shifting roles of, 93–94
    vulnerability in, 7–9
responding to bias, 119–121
risks
    of being yourself, 106–107
    of coming out, calculating,
      59–60
roles, self versus, 89–94
Ross, Loretta, 138
Ruben, Rick, xv

second-guessing yourself, 81–88
self, roles versus, 89–94
self-criticism, 97
self-disclosure, 39–45
self-doubt, 81–88
self-management, 97
sensitivity, 95
setting boundaries. *See* boundaries
shame, in difficult conversations,
    138
sharing pronouns, 31–38. *See also*
    coming out as transgender;
    disclosing
sincerity, 85
situation modification, 97
social media, 143–149
strengths/weaknesses
    identifying, 5–6
    using, 86
Sucher, Sandra J., 57–71
Sumberg, Karen, 106
support system
    in difficult conversations,
      139–140
    in model minority myth, 118–119
    in name misidentification,
      128–129
    in self-doubt, 86–87
surface acting, 76–77
systemic racism, 125–126

talent blindness, 115
transgender, coming out as, 57–71
  advocating for policy changes,
    61–62
  boundaries, setting, 68–69
  calculating risks of, 59–60
  dealing with others' reactions,
    64–66
  mental health management, 63–64
  personal conversations, 62–63
  physical/emotional changes, 66
  recognizing the void, 69–70
  researching information on, 60–61
  spotlight management, 67–68

unconscious bias, 126–127. *See also*
  bias

values, 15–21
  defining, 18–19, 21
  finding, 16–17, 21

  using, 19–20, 21
  well-being and, 134
voice, finding your, 7–9
void, recognizing when coming out as
    transgender, 69–70
Vu, Minh, 112–114
vulnerability, 7–9, 26–27, 28, 66

"want to" thinking, 78
weaknesses/strengths
  identifying, 5–6
  using, 86
weight, stigma about, 48
well-being, values and, 134
Wilding, Melody, 90–91,
    95–101
work self, 26–27
worst-case scenarios, 107
writing name phonetically, 128

Zheng, Lily, 31–38

ABOUT THE CONTRIBUTORS

MADISON BUTLER, chief people officer at Texas-based GRAV, is an outspoken advocate, culture adviser, and speaker. She has been recognized for contributing a bold approach to expanding inclusivity across LGBTQ+ and queer communities while also championing Black and brown entrepreneurs and professionals. Madison is committed to helping change the narrative around what it looks like to be "human at work."

LAN NGUYEN CHAPLIN is a professor of marketing at North-western University's Medill School of Journalism, Media, and Integrated Marketing Communications. She is also the founder of QuanTâm, a nonprofit that creates opportunities for young professionals to expand their networks and sharpen their professional skills while serving their communities.

MICHAEL CHERNY is a senior global leader in diversity, equity, and inclusion. He is a human rights advocate, an active member of the 2SLGBTQ+ community, and an experienced board director. He has been recognized as a Catalyst Canada Honours Champion, a CPA Ontario Emerging Leader, Women in Capital Markets Champion for Change, and Notable Life LGBTQ+ Leader of the Year, and he is a thought leader in the DEI space.

DORIE CLARK is a marketing strategist and a keynote speaker who teaches at Columbia Business School and has been named one of the top 50 business thinkers in the world by Thinkers50. Her latest book is *The Long Game: How to Be a Long-Term Thinker in a Short-Term World* (Harvard Business Review Press, 2021).

PAIGE COHEN (they/them) is a senior editor at *Harvard Business Review*.

IRINA COZMA is a career and executive coach who helps professionals have better career adventures. She has coached hundreds of *Fortune* 500 executives from global organizations like Salesforce, Hitachi, and Abbott. Irina also coaches clients at startups and students in the Physician Executive MBA program at the University of Tennessee. Find her at www.irinacozma .com.

SUSAN DAVID is a founder of the Harvard/McLean Institute of Coaching, is on faculty at Harvard Medical School, and is recognized as one of the world's leading management thinkers. She is the author of the number one *Wall Street Journal* bestseller *Emotional Agility*, which is based on a concept named by *Harvard Business Review* as a management idea of the year. An in-demand speaker and adviser, she has worked with the senior leadership of hundreds of major organizations, including the United Nations, EY, and the World Economic Forum.

DANNIE LYNN FOUNTAIN is a passionate storyteller who helps companies focus on people. By day she's a disability accommodations program manager at Google, hiring the world's most talented software engineers, and by night she supports clients and brands with HR-focused diversity, equity, and inclusion strategies. Beyond working in HR, Dannie Lynn is a six-time author, a licensed enrolled agent, and the founder of the #sidehustlegal movement. She has been interviewed or quoted in the *New York Times*, *Forbes*, *Bustle*, *Bloomberg*, *Business Insider*, *Cosmopolitan*, *Digiday*, the *Everygirl*, *Girlboss*, and more. She is the author of the books *Ending Checkbox Diversity* and *Keep Your Day Job* (forthcoming 2024).

SHALENE GUPTA is a writer and journalist. She's the author of *The Cycle: Confronting the Pain of Periods and PMDD* and a coauthor of *The Power of Trust*.

TUCCI IVOWI is the CEO and a founding member of the Ghana Commodity Exchange. Previously she worked with Nestlé in various roles, including managing director, business executive officer, and marketing communications director, across 22 countries. Her professional experience spans the United Kingdom, emerging markets of Southeast Asia, and sub-Saharan Africa.

AMANDA KERSEY is a senior audio producer at *Harvard Business Review* and the producer of the podcast *Women at Work*.

TALISA LAVARRY is the owner of Morale First, a workplace DEI consultancy, and the author of *Confessions from Your Token Black Colleague*. Tali is also known as America's Anti-Racism Coach. Following her TedX Talk "Your Journey to True Allyship," she published the workbook *Allyship & Me: A Self-Paced, Personal Growth Playbook and Journal* for aspiring allies. From keynotes to workshops to training, coaching, and more, Tali passionately works with her clients to curate sustainable solutions that nurture intrinsic change. Find her on Instagram @americas _anti_racism_coach.

SUSAN MCPHERSON is the founder and CEO of McPherson Strategies and the author of *The Lost Art of Connecting*.

EVELYN NAM is a graduate of Harvard Kennedy School, Columbia Journalism School, and Harvard Divinity School. She has reported on business and Asian American affairs and is an assistant editor at Harvard Business Publishing.

TIM O'BRIEN is a lecturer in public policy at the Harvard Kennedy School, where his work focuses on the gap between the demands of complex challenges and the meaning people bring to them. He teaches Exercising Leadership, a course highlighting the politics of change, and Developing People, focused on adult development. He is also the faculty chair for two Harvard Kennedy School Executive Education programs: Leadership for the 21st Century, for senior executives in government, corporate, and nonprofit organizations; and The Art and Practice of Leadership Development, for experienced leadership development and consulting professionals. Tim also designs and delivers leadership development programs and consults to a range of trisector organizations.

JANICE OMADEKE is the award-winning author of *Mentorship Unlocked*, is a global thought leader and speaker, and was the CEO and founder of the acquired mentorship software company The Mentor Method. Recognized for her distinctive viewpoints on professional development, mentorship, and inclusive entrepreneurship, she has been profiled in leading publications including *Entrepreneur*, *Forbes*, and *Enterprise Magazine*.

TINA OPIE is a sought-after public speaker and an expert in leadership, culture, and DEI. She is also an associate professor of management at Babson College, a visiting scholar at Harvard Business School, and a coauthor of *Shared Sisterhood* (Harvard Business Review Press, 2022).

KATHERINE W. PHILLIPS was the Paul Calello Professor of Leadership and Ethics and the senior vice dean at Columbia Business School. Her research focused on diversity, stereotyping, status, identity management, information sharing, minority influence, decision-making, and performance in work groups.

LUDMILA N. PRASLOVA is the author of *The Canary Code: A Guide to Neurodiversity, Dignity, and Intersectional Belonging at Work*. She uses her extensive experience with neurodiversity and global and cultural inclusion to help create talent-rich workplaces. She is a professor of graduate industrial-organizational psychology and the accreditation liaison officer at Vanguard University of Southern California.

SANDRA J. SUCHER is a professor of management practice at Harvard Business School and a coauthor of *The Power of Trust*.

MELODY WILDING is an executive coach and the author of *Trust Yourself: Stop Overthinking and Channel Your Emotions for Success at Work*.

LILY ZHENG is a DEI strategist, consultant, and speaker who works with organizations to achieve the DEI impact and outcomes they need. They are the author of *DEI Deconstructed*.

Accelerate your career with HBR's Work Smart Series.

If you enjoyed this book and want more career advice from *Harvard Business Review*, turn to other books in **HBR's Work Smart Series**. Each title explores the topics that matter most to you as you start out in your career: being yourself at work, collaborating with (sometimes difficult) colleagues, maintaining your mental health, and more. **HBR's Work Smart Series** books are your go-to guides to step into and move forward successfully in your professional world.

---

store.hbr.org

Buy for your team, clients, or event.
Visit hbr.org/bulksales for quantity discount rates.